# The Great Depression

## Its Impact on Forty-Six Large American Public Libraries

# THE GREAT DEPRESSION: ITS IMPACT ON FORTY-SIX LARGE AMERICAN PUBLIC LIBRARIES, AN INQUIRY BASED ON A CONTENT ANALYSIS OF PUBLISHED WRITINGS OF THEIR DIRECTORS

by
Robert Scott Kramp

A dissertation submitted in partial fulfillment
of the requirements for the degree of
Doctor of Philosophy
(Library Science)
in The University of Michigan
1975

Doctoral Committee:
Professor Rose Vainstein, Chairman
Associate Professor Frank E. Beaver
Associate Professor Rose Mary Magrill
Professor Kenneth E. Vance

Library Juice Press
Duluth, Minnesota

Copyright Robert Scott Kramp, 1975

Published in 2010 by Library Juice Press
P.O. Box 3320
Duluth, MN 55803
http://libraryjuicepress.com/

This book is printed on acid-free paper that meets present ANSI standards for archival preservation.

Library of Congress Cataloging-in-Publication Data

Kramp, Robert Scott.
 The Great Depression : its impact on forty-six large American public libraries : an inquiry based on a content analysis of published writings of their directors / by Robert Scott Kramp.
     p. cm.
 Originally presented as the author's thesis (Ph. D.)--University of Michigan, 1975.
 Includes bibliographical references and index.
 ISBN 978-1-936117-02-4 (acid-free paper)
 1. Public libraries--United States--History--20th century. 2. Libraries and society--United States--History--20th century. 3. United States--Social conditions--1918-1932. 4. United States--Social conditions--1933-1945. 5. United States--Economic conditions--1918-1945. I. Title.
 Z731.K69 2010
 021.20973--dc22
                                                2010006993

# Contents

| | |
|---|---|
| Dedication | vii |
| Acknowledgements | ix |
| **Chapter 1: Statement of the Problem** | 1 |
| Historical Background | |
| **Chapter 2: Review of Related Research** | 25 |
| Doctoral Dissertations | |
| Books, Articles, Reports, 1930-1940 | |
| **Chapter 3: Review of Related Research** | 51 |
| **Chapter 4: Findings Based on Content Analysis** | 61 |
| Introduction | |
| Source of Comment | |
| Comment on Categories: Categories Receiving Major Attention, Categories Relating to the Library in Its Socio-Political Setting, Categories Relating to Economic Conditions | |
| Comment on Time-Span, Source, and Director Attitude toward Material | |
| Major Contributors to the Universe: Harry Miller Lydenberg, Clarence Sherman, Milton J. Ferguson, George F. Bowerman, Ralph Munn, Judson Jennings, Milton Lord, Carl Roden, Adam Strohm, Malcolm Wyer, Harold Brigham, Charles C. Compton, Carl Vitz | |
| **Chapter 5: Results and Recommendations** | 123 |
| Appendices | 145 |
| Bibliography | 147 |
| Index | 153 |

To my wife

## Acknowledgements

The author's gratitude to all of the people and institutions whose efforts were essential to the completion of the study can never be adequately expressed. Even a list of major contributors is long.

Four libraries, those of The University of Michigan and the University of Illinois, as well as the Michigan State Library and the Detroit Public Library, supplied the primary and secondary material on which the study is based. The author's employer, Oakland Schools, and its staff supplied much. Dr. William J. Emerson, Superintendent, gave administrative support and encouragement. Dr. William Veitch provided computer programs that counted and tabulated the data once they had been coded. Dr. Roy J. Butz tested the accuracy of the technique by recording a sample of the author's work. The staff of Oakland Schools' Library discharged many of the author's duties when his work on the study kept him from those duties.

Three people, Mrs. Ellen Oliver, Mrs. Norine Isgrigg, and the dedicatee, typed the drafts and the final copy, often working with difficult deadlines. In addition to typing much of the material, the dedicatee also supplied editorial counsel and assistance, encouraged the author, and for a time, supported him and their family at the beginning of this course of study. To Sylvia Camu Kramp and to our children, I am grateful.

Finally, the doctoral committee contributed far more to the successful completion of this effort than the author had any right to hope for. Professor Rose Mary Magrill provided research expertise and advice on literary style. Professor Frank E. Beaver contributed the essential knowledge of content analysis as well as continuous encouragement. Professor Kenneth E. Vance brought technical expertise and stylistic judgment to the committee. And its chairman, Professor Rose Vainstein, deserves special thanks for helping shape the dissertation in its scholarship, style, presentation, and form. Her unfailing, yet exacting, guidance, patience, and encouragement made the completion of the dissertation possible.

To all of these institutions and people, the author recognizes his debt. He claims for himself only one thing, responsibility for the errors that have survived the efforts of so many to find them.

*Chapter 1*
Statement of the Problem

Introduction

The scholarly writing on the economic depression that began at the time of the stock market crash of 1929 and ended with our arming for World War II is voluminous and covers every conceivable aspect of its economic, political, and social phases. From its onset up to the present time, the depression has commanded the attention of historians, economists, politicians, sociologists, educators, and all other scholars. Every time a recession or an economic downturn hits the economy, fresh interest is rekindled in the subject of the depression, and comparisons are made using it as a measure of the severity of the nation's economic ills. Yet in all this writing over a period of about forty years, very little treats how the public library functioned as a public institution during the depression.

Four major historians who are the acknowledged authorities on the depression are Arthur Meier Schlesinger, Jr., William E. Leuchtenberg, Broadus Mitchell, and Dixon Wecter. In their writings, only one of them, Dixon Wecter, mentions the public library. Schlesinger, Leuchtenberg, and Mitchell seem largely unaware that the public library fulfilled a social, psychological and educational role in the lives of the people during the depression.

Schlesinger, in writing nearly nineteen hundred pages about the depression, devotes one hundred sixty of them to bibliography or to bibliographic footnotes. His study, the largest on the subject, attempts to treat all phases of the depression, primarily those of social and political significance. The last pages of Volume One foreshadow much that he says in subsequent volumes.

> The American experiment in self-government was now facing what was, excepting the Civil War, its greatest test [...] And through the world the free way of life was already in retreat [...] Many had deserted freedom, many more had lost their nerve [...] the collapse of the older order meant catharsis rather than catastrophe; [...] catastrophe could provide the indispensable setting for democratic experiment and for presidential leadership. If this were so, then crisis could change from calamity to challenge.[1]

In his study of the impact of the depression on American political life, Leuchtenberg supplies a similarly impressive bibliography: fifteen pages of formal bibliography are supplemented by nearly one thousand footnotes, this is a volume of fewer than four hundred pages. Not one has a reference to the impact of the depression on libraries. Leucthenberg assesses the impact of the depression on American life and measures the government's role in helping cushion that impact.

> For the first time for many Americans, the federal government became an institution that was directly experienced. More than state or local governments, it came to be the government, an agency directly concerned with their welfare. It was the source of their relief payments; it taxed them directly for old age pensions;

---

[1] Arthur Meier Schlesinger, Jr., *Age of Roosevelt*, 3 Vols. (Boston: Riverside Press of Houghton Mifflin, 1957-60), I, pp. 484-85.

CHAPTER ONE 3

it even gave their children hot lunches in school. As the role of the state changed from that of neutral arbiter to a "powerful promoter of society's welfare," people felt an interest in Washington they never had before.[2]

Mitchell's study of the economic consequences of the depression is equally well-documented: he has four hundred footnotes and thirty pages of formal bibliography.[3] Mitchell attempts to summarize the economic history of the period as reflected through the actions of the Roosevelt administration. Yet neither Leuchtenberg nor Mitchell treats the impact of the library on American society during the period, nor do they mention the effect that the depression had on libraries.

Finally, Dixon Wecter attempts to study everything, from the economic causes to the attempts at amelioration and to the social and cultural implications of the depression. And alone of these major historians, Wecter has a comment about libraries:

> Idle millions discovered the public library as the poor man's club, a warm quiet place to browse or drowse. The American Library Association estimated in 1933 that between three and four million new borrowers had been added since 1929, while the total circulation

---

[2] William E. Leuchtenberg, *Franklin D. Roosevelt and the New Deal, 1929-41*, New American Nation Series (New York: Harper and Row, 1963), p. 331.

[3] Broadus Mitchell, *Depression Decade: From New Era Through New Deal, 1929-41,* Economic History of the United States Series Vol. IX, First Torchbook Edition (New York: Harper and Row, 1969).

of books had increased nearly forty percent [...] Unhappily, however, at this moment of greatest opportunity, library authorities groaned under a burden of poverty. In sixty large cities book buying funds dwindled from an annual two and a third million dollars in 1931 to less than a million in 1933. The Chicago Library, in the exposition year when that city strove to put its best foot forward, faced its third consecutive season with no book funds whatsoever.[4]

His comments on public libraries are contained in two paragraphs less than a page long in a history of 362 pages. As will be discussed at greater length in Chapter II of this study, Wecter did not have a large body of published material on which to base his remarks about libraries. His only cited source is a non-scholarly work by a popular writer, Robert L. Duffus, who wrote the only generally available treatment of libraries of varying sizes all over the United States and then commented on what those public libraries were suffering as a result of the economic chaos of the period.[5]

Thus, there is a need for scholarly treatment by historians of the public library during the depression, for the public library was itself a social and political institution that contributed much to the public during that time and should have its place in the history of the depression. It is, therefore, the purpose of this study to provide information to historians and other scholars on how the depression affected large public libraries and perhaps provide the

---

[4] Dixon Wecter, *Age of the Great Depression, 1929-41,* New York: Macmillan Company, 1948), p. 244.
[5] Robert L. Duffus, *Our Starving Libraries* (Boston: Houghton Mifflin. 1933).

groundwork for the writing of a history of the depression's effect on public libraries.

*Objectives*

This study assessed the impact of the depression on large public libraries in the United States through the use of content analysis. It analyzes the depression-related writings of the directors of the forty-six American public libraries that served more than 200,000 people on census day, 1 April, 1930 and focuses on the categories of subject matter related to the depression that the directors wrote about. The study's four main objectives are: (1) to study the impact of the depression on the internal operations of the libraries, (2) to find how and where the depression affected library services, (3) to learn whether library policies changed as a result of the depression, and (4) to find whether directors of public libraries changed their attitudes regarding their libraries, the public, or any other matter as a result of the depression.

*(1) To study the impact of the depression on the internal operations of the library*

One can assume staff changes as a result of budget reductions; one can also venture the hypothesis that changes conducive to the streamlining of organization were attempted. To see whether that hypothesis is accurate and to find if other changes in internal operations were deliberately made to adjust to the impact of the depression are initial objectives of the study.

*(2) To find how and where the depression affected library services*

One can assume that as a result of straitened finances, many libraries were forced to curtail some services, especially those requiring personnel who could no longer be paid. An initial phase of this objective is to see which services were eliminated first, and what priorities existed in the retention of others. As a corollary part of this objective, an effort is made to determine whether any director added any services that were badly needed despite the lack of money. Again, attention is paid to the addition of one service at the expense of another.

*(3) To learn whether library policies changed as a result of the depression*

The study was undertaken with the belief that the directors of libraries would discuss their deliberations on matters of policy, and that the discussions would appear in both annual reports and journal articles.

*(4) To find whether directors of public libraries changed their attitudes regarding their libraries, the public, or any other matter as a result of the depression*

To the end of finding useful information here, all of the directors' writings in annual reports and journals during the depression were studied. An initial surmise was that events and changes that affected them would elicit their reactions in their writings.

The depression was a common reality to be faced by the public library directors. All were confronted with the problems of reduced finances, reduced staff, greater demands for books and services, and other problems. It is to be expected that they would report on their problems in annual reports and that they would share common concerns with library colleagues in the journals.

The objectives may be summarized thus: since the depression had an impact on public libraries and forced library directors to discuss common problems and concerns, the objectives are to find what subjects they discussed and what they said, where they agreed or disagreed and the amount of attention that they devoted to each of their concerns.

*Assumptions*

The assumptions relate necessarily to methodology: content analysis imposes assumptions on those who use it. Those assumptions relate to the universe, which in this study is composed of the body of writings of the public library directors of the forty-six libraries in annual reports and selected journals.

First, it is assumed that the directors said what they wanted and intended to say, and that their concerns were not distorted by pressures from their boards or publics. The study could not have proceeded without the assumption that the directors were always speaking solely for themselves: assigning any other motivations to their comments would be beyond the scope of the study.

Second, it must be assumed that somewhere in the universe is all the material that is relevant to the study and that the directors stated everything they wanted to say in their annual reports and in articles written for library periodicals. This assumption is equally questionable but equally necessary. If the study is to be manageable, newspaper articles, correspondence, aides-memoires, and the like have to be ruled out, for the mere task of retrieving them to see if they are relevant to the subject would make the total effort limitless.

Third, everything that appeared over the name of the director in annual reports or in committee reports is to be considered his own work. This assumption is not as serious a weakness as it might appear. Although a director may not have produced the text, he would not have allowed an article or a report to appear over his name if he had disagreed with it in any way. In this regard, the director is as much the author of published statements as the President of the United Sates is the author of speeches whose content is worked out by a committee and whose exact text is supplied by an anonymous wordsmith. He must subsequently defend the speech's content and phraseology, and when bibliographic responsibility is assigned, it is assigned either to him or to his office.

The final three assumptions can be treated quickly, for in a sense, they derive from the first three. Fourth, there is a relationship between the volume of materials in a category and that category's importance to the directors. Fifth, comparisons made on the basis of these quantities can be taken seriously. Sixth, content analysis, as well as aiding in testing the hypotheses listed below, may well generate further hypotheses for even more sophisticated testing.

*Hypotheses*

The hypotheses were tested by the technique of content analysis. The universe was determined, categories were generated, and the content in the universe was analyzed according to the categories. The main purpose in choosing content analysis was to use a methodology that would eliminate investigator bias in the examination of available evidence and to test hypotheses meaningful in discussing public libraries during a depression. To this end, the following hypotheses were selected:

1. That the economic depression of the nineteen thirties directly affected the public library, its services, operations, and policies.

2. That public library directors made adjustments in services, operations and role to enable the library to stay within available revenue and so far as possible, to meet changing needs.

3. That both federal and state governmental activity elicited an increasing volume of written response from public library directors.

4. That the depression affected the attitude of public library directors toward the role of the public library as an institution and toward the public.

*Limitations*

As was indicated in the *Assumptions* section above, limitations of a variety of sorts had to be applied to the study in order to hold it within workable limits. In addition to those that involved assumptions, three others had to be applied: time period, sources, and universe.

The time period had to be given beginning and ending dates, even though there is no consensus on the exact dates when the depression began and ended. Typically, the fiscal years and the annual reports began on 1 July and ended on 30 June. For purposes of this study, 1 January 1930 was the beginning point of the depression and 31 December 1940 was the ending point. In fact, there were no substantial contributions before 1930 or after 1940. Even though we were not to be involved in World War II for nearly another full year, arming for it had relieved much unemployment, many other indexes of economic activity had turned upward, and library directors had turned their thoughts from the calamity of the depression to the calamity of war.

For purposes of this study, the year 1929 was not especially significant. No articles appeared treating economic conditions and no public library directors mentioned them in their annual reports, despite the fact that by the time of the stock market crash in October 1929, evidence had already attested to an economic downturn. For example, Galbraith said:

> According to the accepted view of events by the autumn of 1929, the economy was well into a depression. In June the indexes of industrial and of factory production both reached a peak and turned down. By October, the Federal Reserve index of industrial production stood at 117 as compared with 126 four months earlier. Steel production declined from June on; in October freight-car loadings fell. Homebuilding, a most mercurial industry, had been falling for several years, and it slumped still further in 1929. Finally, down came the stock market [...][6]

---

[6] John Kenneth Galbraith, *The Great Crash, 1929,* Sentry Edition (Boston: Riverside Press of Houghton Mifflin, 1961), p. 93.

The sources were selected with the thought of using the material produced by those concerned with administering, working in, or being employed by large public libraries. In order to limit the sample of those whose writing would most likely be widely read, chief administrators of large public libraries were chosen. As a further limitation, only directors serving libraries in the American Library Association's largest size grouping, that is libraries serving more than 200,000 persons, were selected. [7]

Finally, the universe was limited to the director's contributions to their libraries' annual reports and to their articles in nine journals: the *American Library Association Bulletin*, *Journal of Adult Education*, *Libraries*, *Library Journal*, *Library Quarterly*, *Publishers' Weekly*, *School and Society*, *Special Libraries*, and *Wilson Bulletin for Librarians*. [8] Annual reports used were those in The University of Michigan Library, and library of The University of Illinois, and The Detroit Public Library. [9]

---

[7] See Appendix I-A, pp. 145-48.

[8] Two principles governed this selection of journals: their nationwide circulation and the broad professional interest in the matters treated in them.

[9] These three libraries are acknowledged scholarly libraries in the area; each has lacunae in its collection of annual reports, but each has attempted to fill in gaps by limited distribution during the depression period.

## Historical Background

*Introduction*

To the extent that the events of the depression influenced the actions of the public libraries during the period and to the extent that comment on those events is accessible, it is appropriate for this dissertation to consider briefly what some of those events were. Presumably, the public library as the people's forum and university was similar to other popular institutions in reflecting the effect of popular attitudes, trends, government agencies, and cultural movements. It is to be expected, for instance, that in a time of crisis such as the depression was, an upsurge of radicalism would characterize the actions of the people.[10] It did not occur. Other events that can be attributed to the depression did occur, however, and it is the purpose of this section of the study to discuss some of them, however briefly, and to point toward a few of the historians whose works have provided the bulk of the information that follows.

*The Depression*

The passage of three decades has pretty well assured agreement that the depression occurred and that its dates were about as indicated in the *Limitations* section above. Within the decade, however, there were fluctuations in the severity of the depression. Mitchell cities three major phases through which the period passed:

---

[10] Leuchtenberg, p. 15.

CHAPTER ONE 13

> Without an attempt or to explain the relatively minor ups and downs, it may be said that there were three major trends of roughly equal duration. The first was a fairly steady decline for three years and ten months, until the low point was reached on March 18, 1933, with the index at 63.7. The second phase, covering three years and ten months, was that of apparent recovery, to the middle of August 1937. The three years and three months in length, began with precipitate "recession" becoming irregular improvements...[11]

Each of the phases was accompanied by a distinct effect on public library services and budgets, as will be developed later.[12] One may assume that public librarians paid a certain amount of attention to government-supported remedies to problems, especially after the inauguration of Franklin D. Roosevelt in March 1933. Directors can also be expected to have paid attention to many of the work-relief programs, to have commented on those that were effective and to have criticized those that fell short of their promise.

*Presidential Action*

Franklin D. Roosevelt was the dominant figure of the decade. The goals and performance of agencies originated by his administration commanded more of the attention of the historians of the decade that any other facet of his administration. Mitchell's lengthy sketch of the foci of the programs divides Roosevelt's efforts to cope with

---

[11] Mitchell, p. 93.
[12] See Chapter IV, pp. 64-67, 70-73.

the depression into four stages.[13] In the first phase, from 1933-1935, Roosevelt tried to control business, an effort that foundered when the Supreme Court invalidated vital parts of the Agricultural Adjustment Act and the National Industrial Recovery Act in 1935 and 1936. The second phase, from 1936-1937, was, according to Mitchell, characterized by pump priming, an attempt to infuse new life into business by governmental actions, loans, and support. This welfare-for-business was drastically reduced in 1937, bringing on the third period. During the third phase, from 1937-1939, the recession that was brought on by the abandonment of the pump priming efforts of the second phase was blamed by the administration on the forces of the business community. New relief programs were not attempted; new agencies did not try to cope with the new economic problems caused by deficit spending and the price-raising policies practiced earlier. Instead, the administration investigated business, futilely blaming it for all of the country's ills. In the fourth phase, from 1939-1940, arming for the Second World War ended concern for economic problems. A number of programs begun in the second phase, notably the Works Progress Administration, the National Youth Administration, the Civil Works Administration, and the Public Works Administration, continued until remaining in 1940 obviated them.

The impact of the depression was felt even before the inauguration of Roosevelt; in fact, he was elected because people felt he could deal with their depression problems while Hoover could not. Actually, despite popular notion to the contrary, many commentators have credited Roosevelt's success to his ability to copy models left over from

---

[13] Mitchell, pp. 405-07.

the term of President Hoover. However, during his term of office, Hoover did not learn immediately how to cope with the depression. For a long time, he felt that the federal government should not involve itself in relief efforts, these being the proper province of the states, and for the federal government to supersede the status in the matter would in the long run weaken the states and be counterproductive. He had similar feelings about government involvement in business. Eventually, as the depression worsened and the states and business became more and more paralyzed, Hoover reversed his stand. But by then, as Hicks points out, Hoover's efforts were not equal to the task of reversing international economic trends.[14]

As Hoover's economic policies failed, the Democratic Party approached the 1932 presidential nominating conventions with growing certainty that its next nominee would be elected. Broadus Mitchell commented that the economy was continuing to weaken. A temporary upturn had occurred in the summer of 1932 but it did not help the Republican Party's chances in the election. And yet, with all the economic turmoil and distress, Leutchenberg observes:

> At both conventions the delegates showed far more concern over prohibition than over unemployment. "Here we are," wrote John Dewey, "in the midst of the greatest crisis since the Civil War and the only thing the two national parties seem to want to debate is booze." The Democrats, who had been torn apart by the liquor issue in the twenties, determined that this would not happen again. It was ridiculous, observed a

---

[14] John Hicks, *Republican Ascendency*, 1921-33, New American Nation Series (New York: Harper and Row, 1960), pp. 234-35.

Missourian, for a jobless wet Democrat to wrangle with a jobless dry Democrat over liquor when neither could afford the price of a drink...[15]

*Popular Reactions*

A number of forces coalesced in the winter of 1932-33 to make it the worst of the depression. No governmental efforts at amelioration had availed anything. The discredited Hoover administration could not compel a recalcitrant Congress to act; the incoming administration would neither endorse nor attack any of the Hoover proposals; the closing of the banks had endangered what savings the Americans still had not used; and no solutions seemed to work.

Questions were raised which indicated distrust of business and the American capitalistic system,[16] but radicals failed to score any gains in the 1932 elections. After three years of depression under a Republican administration, the Democrats, as might be expected, gained an overwhelming ninety seats in the House and thirteen in the Senate. But the performance of the radicals was insignificant for neither the Communists nor the socialists attracted many votes.[17]

As soon as he was inaugurated, President Roosevelt immediately took steps to alleviate some of the physical and psychic suffering of the people. His relief programs became New Deal attempts to force money to circulate among some of the most desperate of the unemployed.

---

[15] Leutchenberg, p. 9.
[16] Ibid., p. 27.
[17] Ibid., p. 122.

His initial effort in work-relief was the Civil Works Administration which gave many CWA workers and their families their first opportunity in months to pay for the bare essentials for survival; food, necessary goods, fuel for warmth during the record-breaking cold winter of 1933, where for millions of workers only the CWA provided the margin of relief from cold and want.[18]

The questions for which the government had no answers and the enforced leisure time had been sending people to the libraries in unprecedented millions in 1931 and 1932. Their presence there, as will be described in Chapters IV and V, was the basis of much comment among directors. Similarly, library directors discussed the reduction in demands for library service as economic conditions improved during the first Roosevelt administration. The dramatic increase in service requests after the end of pump priming in the early months of the second administration brought the most worried comments of all. When the economy weakened the second time, in 1937, the administration that had corrected matters in 1933 seemed powerless. The population that had learned in 1933 to look to Washington for help now learned that the Roosevelt administration was unable or unwilling to help. Library directors were not radically different from the people they served. They also learned to think of the federal government as a source of succor in time of need, and this attitude was reflected in their writings.

---

[18] Ibid.

*The Government Agencies*

One of the agencies of government that originated during the New Deal is still with us; the Tennessee Valley Authority (TVA) is an outstanding example of a worthwhile agency from the depression that survived. The Public Works Administration (PWA) provided a federal architecture to contrast with the federalist buildings of an earlier period. Examples of both are still extant. But many of the other agencies left few permanent memorials and went out of existence when the economic emergency ended.

The Civilian Conservation Corp (CCC), which sent unemployed youths into the woods for six months on reforestation projects, was a popular agency. Its back-to-the-land orientation had an inescapable appeal that the urban-oriented agencies did not share. Popular myth claimed that the urban agencies were founded to hire people to rake leaves, count traffic, and lean on shovels.

Among the relief agencies that hired people to do jobs on short notice were the Civil Works Administration (CWA) and the Federal Emergency Relief Administration (FERA), its predecessor. These agencies shared a disadvantage in that they were hastily established to provide temporary emergency employment in a crisis and could offer local sponsoring groups little time to plan the work the new employees were to do. Thus, abundant evidence of bad planning accumulated, especially where untrained, nearly unsupervised people were thrown into tasks for which some training and direction were required under the best circumstances. Library programs under FERA and CWA were often good in that the workers were set to cleaning books and buildings, to typing according to simple instructions, and to other easily supervised and taught tasks.[19] The National Youth Administration (NYA) also provided students who worked as library pages.

The Works Progress Administration (WPA), the best-known and perhaps the most effective of the New Deal relief agencies, supplied jobs to the otherwise unemployed and labor to public agencies whose budgets had been so severely curtailed by depression-forced reductions that damaging cutbacks in programs had resulted and would have been worse but for the WPA labor. Mitchell's description of the limitations on the program indicates how it could operate. A WPA project had to have local sponsors; the project had to be useful to the public; it could not interfere with private enterprise; WPA workers had to be able to do the job; it had to be labor-intensive; it had to be capable of completion within the fiscal year; and, usually, it had to be on public property.[20]

Just as the depression had sent many desperate people in droves to the library for reading material—either for escape or for vocational training—now the government had sent them to the libraries for employment on WPA jobs to relieve their despair. Many of them came to regard themselves as government employees, not as relief workers.[21] Government employees or relief workers, they contributed to the economies of the libraries wherein they worked. For the library budgets had been reduced by the depression, the staff cuts had been crippling, and the workers provided by the WPA were a great help.[22]

---

[19] See Chapter II, pp. 25-28.
[20] Mitchell, pp. 330-31.
[21] Wecter, p. 96.
[22] See Chapter IV, pp. 62-64.

Finally, by establishing codes of fair competition, the National Recovery Administration (NRA) tried to end the ruinous competition that had accompanied the early depression efforts of many businesses to stay in business. By the time of the Schecter decision in 1935, which effectively ended the NRA by invalidating its claim to regulate interstate commerce by establishing codes of fair competition, a right that the Supreme Court ruled belonged only to the Congress and could not be delegated to an administrative agency, the NRA had created a number of problems for the libraries of the nation. Both book producers and book sellers agreed under their codes to end practices that libraries had long utilized to buy more books than their budgets would have permitted, the most notable being the use of discounts; publishers and jobbers agreed to end them. Strangely, there was little comment on NRA and its codes from the library directors in this sample. It may be worth noting, however, that the blue eagle, a logo symbolizing cooperation with the appropriate NRA codes, disappeared from the *Library Journal* editorial page as soon after the Schecter decision of 27, May 1935 as was humanly possible. The work relief programs of the New Deal of the Roosevelt administration gave work, usefulness, a means of livelihood, a dignity to millions of people who built and repaired buildings, schools, playgrounds, bridges, roads, viaducts, bandstands, airports, parks, waterways, hospitals, courthouses, swimming pools, sewers, and privies and who did a multitude of tasks. The programs were important in the lives of the people of the United States during the depression and helped them survive. They were helpful to the libraries as well by providing needed labor in public libraries.

CHAPTER ONE 21

*The Society*

Discussions of the depression period must begin with the government and politics. This study has done so. In the next few pages, the extent of the popular response to economic events, governmental activity, and the interplay of the two will be discussed to whatever limited extent is necessary as background to the events in the library world.

One of the social issues raised about the depression was whether it fostered the growth of radicalism during the decade. The redhunts of the late forties and the early fifties encouraged the myth that there were several red cells on every university campus, in every governmental jurisdiction, and, one guesses, on nearly every city block. The falsity of the myth is indicated by the elections. At no time did the Communists win, and the Midwest Progressives did no better than they had done for decades.[23]

The size of the following of such leaders as Dr. Francis Townsend, Senator Huey Long, and Fr. Charles Coughlin collectively numbered in the millions, and indicated potential power that could have strongly influenced either the government or the society if it had ever been stirred to joint action. The murder of Senator Long ended any political threat the groups may have had. The Townsendites and the followers of Fr. Coughlin were not so organized as to constitute a power base for either a political or social leader. From among the followers of the three and from among the rest of an America that recognized an opportunity to right some long-standing wrongs came the

---

[23] Leuchtenberg, p. 27.

members of the only really potent organizations to emerge from the depression—the unions.

The overthrow of the National Industrial Recovery Act in 1935 temporarily troubled the supporters of labor organizations, for one of its provisions had been a guarantee of the rights to organize and to strike. But the Wagner Act (or the National Labor Relations Act) of 1935 reestablished those guarantees, leading to the growth of American labor unions, even in a few libraries. The threat of such growth, or its promise, depending on one's viewpoint, excited librarians to comment that will be discussed at length later in this dissertation.[24]

Communism, while never a potent political force during the decade, attracted a fairly large group of what Schlesinger characterized as the "...lower intelligentsia [...] the discontented magazine writer, the guilty Hollywood scenarist, the aggrieved university instructor, the underpaid high school teacher, [...] the culturally aspiring dentist for whom Marxism as a system of [...] consolation carried great appeal".[25] These people could be expected to haunt the libraries, demanding the latest in their new-found areas of interest. Apart from a growing number of requests for materials in the social sciences, however, the directors did not report demands for the vituperative and controversial books written on the tenets of Marx.

Finally, during the decade, there was a growth of concern about civil rights, especially for Negroes, who were for the first time being given equal treatment in many

---

[24] See Chapter IV, pp.80-82.
[25] Schlesinger, III, p. 165.

New Deal programs.[26] The concern did not extend to the libraries, where reports of southern libraries talked of the Negro branch that typically provided library service to Negro citizens with smaller collections, fewer hours, and smaller budgets per capita than did the central library and the branches reserved for the white citizens who used the library irrespective of class. Treatment of the Negroes of any group broke into professional print only once, when at the American Library Association's 1936 conference, held in Richmond, Virginia, Negro librarians were accorded inferior treatment. Then, a rash of letters to the *Library Journal* protested the Association's action that put these members in good standing into a compromised position.

*Summary*

The depression had an effect on the functioning of large public libraries from 1930 to 1940, and it is the intention of this dissertation to assess that effect through the use of content analysis. Numerous governmental actions and programs were instituted to counteract the depression's economic effects on the lives of the people, and some of those actions involved the public libraries. The people used the public library more and more as the depression deepened, and gradually left it as they returned to work when the economic conditions improved.

The libraries offered reading material, a place to sit, adult education, some vocational guidance, and sometimes a place to work for those on federal projects. It ful-

---

[26] Leuchtenberg, pp. 185-8.

filled a function in the lives of the people and the society during the depression.

## Chapter 2
## Review of Related Research

Several kinds of material are important in the discussion of works related to the subject matter of this study. Three doctoral dissertations as well as books, journal articles, and reports were written either during or shortly after the decade, 1930-1940, on the general subject of public library survival of depression-created problems or public library reaction to depression-created trends.

*Doctoral Dissertations*

Margaret M. Herdman's dissertation, "The Public Library in Depression",[27] was largely an examination of statistical relationships for the years 1930-1935, with primary emphasis on the relationships between library budgets and numerous cost-cutting efforts, thus echoing the earlier findings of Waples, Carnovsky, and Randall.[28] In her sample of 150 libraries of all sizes, from those serving 2,500 people to those serving over 500,000, Herdman found that as budgets fell salaries declined less dramatically than did total expenditures, but that book expenditures were reduced far more sharply than total expenditures.[29] Other items, such as maintenance and binding,

---

[27] Margaret M. Herdman, "Public Library in Depression" (Ph.D. dissertation, University of Chicago, 1941).
[28] Douglas Waples, Leon Carnovsky, and William M. Randall, "Public Library in Depression," *Library Quarterly*, II, 4 (October 1932): pp. 321-42.
[29] Herdman, pp.25-28, 104.

that represented smaller percentages of total expenditure, were also less hard hit.[30] Overall, a thirteen percent decrease in expenditures occurred during the period she investigated. [31]

She then explored, in detail, the relationship between unemployment and various types of library circulation, finding that during the early years of the depression, from 1930 to 1935, juvenile circulation increased 16 percent and then dropped about 20 percent, juvenile nonfiction increased 20 percent and then dropped a like amount.[32] In adult circulation, fiction showed early gains, although losses in 1934 and 1935 offset them. Non-fiction showed losses also, but they were less spectacular and followed increases that exceeded 40 percent.[33] Adult non-fiction circulation also demonstrated the largest gains, in proportion to other types of material, where it was most available and where the depression had hit the hardest.[34]

Among Herdman's other findings were the facts that book stores decreased in sales and number during the depression, but that book rental agencies increased, that the number of radios available increased 170 percent from 1930 to 1935 (this trend not being related to decrease in circulation), and that the increasing popularity of the movies probably had in relation to the decline in circulation after 1932 and 1933, the drop probably being caused by decreasing book expenditures.[35]

---

[30] Ibid., pp. 33-34.
[31] Ibid., pp. 23.
[32] Ibid., p. 11.
[33] Ibid., p. 11.
[34] Ibid., p. 13-14.
[35] Ibid., pp. 67-68.

CHAPTER TWO 27

Perhaps Herdman's most useful finding was that cost per volume circulated data could not provide reliable measures of library efficiency. This data, she showed, were too volatile to be trusted during times of sever economic distress.[36] Reviewing the pattern of expenditure in her sample of libraries, she found that while expenditures had dropped as much as 23 percent in 1933, by 1935 a quarter to a third of the cuts had been restored.[37]

Herdman devoted her final pages to conclusions in areas of concern to library directors. First, as was just indicated, she claimed that cost per volume circulated was not a reliable index of efficiency. Other conclusions were that book purchases should continue even at the expense of the salary budget, that a wider range of services must be supplied to adults, that medium-sized libraries were hurt less by budget reductions than larger, more rigid institutions or than smaller, totally elastic libraries, that cooperative services should be studied and developed, and that considerable attention must be given to the measurement of services and their components.[38]

Herdman's dissertation synthesized previously scattered studies of the effects of budget cuts on library expenditures and related general unemployment to library circulation.[39] She did not study the impact of the depression on the thinking of librarians nor on the libraries during the second half of the decade, from 1936 to 1940.

Edward Barrett Stanford studied selected programs of the Works Progress Administration as early experiments

---

[36] Ibid., pp. 75-77.
[37] Ibid., p. 79.
[38] Ibid., pp.77-87.
[39] Ibid., pp. 60-62.

in federal aid to libraries, saying early in his dissertation that the results of such programs were clouded by their basic non-library characteristics.[40] The WPA, an agency devoted principally to providing employment for people who were out of work as a result of the depression, had little interest in libraries as such.

The WPA followed the Federal Emergency Relief Administration and the Civil Works Administration in offering uncomplicated, low-level jobs to the otherwise unemployed. Unlike the FERA and WPA, however, its programs eventually assumed a social importance beyond relieving financial want, for the first widespread federal efforts to subsidize local efforts at library service were via the WPA.[41] The report by Professor Carleton Joeckel of the University of Chicago Graduate Library School to the President's Advisory Committee on Education (or, more popularly, the Reeves Committee) had recommended about $17,000,000 in federal support to libraries annually;[42] the WPA support of library services averaged that amount annually between 1936 and 1941.[43]

Initially, the WPA program suffered from lack of planning, from the lack of ability at the federal level to require intelligent control at the state level of WPA library pro-

---

[40] Edward Barrett Stanford, "Libraries Extension under the WPA: An Appraisal of an Early Experiment in Federal Aid" (Ph.D. dissertation, University of Chicago, 1942), p. 1.
[41] Ibid.
[42] Carleton B. Joeckel, *Library Service*, President's Advisory Committee on Education, Staff Study Number 11, (Washington, D.C.; United States Government Printing Office, 1938), p. 83.
[43] Stanford, p. 255.

CHAPTER TWO 29

grams, and from the inefficiency generated by the absence of a good overall library plan. WPA programs often competed with the local programs they were supposed to supplement. There were some inequitable resource allocations and some opposition in established libraries where personnel thought the programs were more troubled than they were worth. Stanford believed that the program, although burdened by these problems, still made notable achievements.[44]

First, the upper echelon administration and coordination of the library efforts themselves were good. Stanford indicates that federal advice, where accepted, produced effective state programs and that often, though not uniformly, state program planning and coordination were good. Second, the importance of generating local interest in, and support for, the WPA projects and demonstration contributed to their success. Third, WPA programs reversed a previous trend in federal projects, which had encouraged the existence of small, weak, independent local libraries. The WPA required that project service areas be large enough so that local support would be adequate to maintain service after the termination of federal support. And fourth, the projects, though staffed largely with the unemployed, had well-trained staffs who were also required to attempt to improve the job performance of the temporary employees.[45]

Finally, Stanford believed that the WPA efforts could serve as a model for other federal library aid programs and that libraries should use the war period (he wrote in

---

[44] Ibid., pp. 261-63.
[45] Ibid., pp. 264-65.

1942) to develop plans based on the strengths and weaknesses of the WPA programs.

Stanford recommended the following: strong state technical authority over library aspects of federal-aid programs, state level authority over their administration, recruitment of competent people (not necessarily limited to the unemployed), insistence on larger, more efficient units of organization, phasing out of federal funds from the demonstration projects, and no requirement that any federal funds be restricted to the hiring of personnel.[46] If one adds the implied requirement that the programs be restricted to the rural (i.e., otherwise unserved) areas of the nation, one has a close parallel to the rules under which the first Library Services Act money was distributed in the late 1950s.

The most important immediate effects of the WPA program can be summarized quickly. Other federal funds supported $50,000,000 in library construction and repair that probably would not have happened otherwise; the total of federal WPA library funds was $100,000,000; twice annual expenditures exceeded the total that Joeckel indicated would be necessary to raise federal support for libraries to a minimum sixty cents per capita, using federal funds to supplement average local efforts.[47]

Stanford, then, was not writing a history of the depression's impact on libraries but rather was studying the effect of one federal program, the works Progress Administration, on one library goal: federal support for library service.

---

[46] Ibid., pp. 265-68.
[47] Ibid., pp. 254-56.

Robert H. Deily investigated the relationship between library support and four variables: 1) the form of municipal government, 2) the sources of revenue (special tax versus appropriation), 3) the "general goodness" of life in cities as defined by E. L. Thorndike, and 4) the proportion of the Negro population. He found that the highest correlation was between "general goodness" and library expenditures, a correlation higher than that between economic ability and library support.[48]

The finding, that there was less correlation between economic ability and library support, Deily derived the inference that many cities do not spend all that they could afford for the support of libraries and other permissive functions (recreation being another) and that they will probably not increase support for one until they improve support for all. His conclusion was that the permissive services have to undertake mutual cooperative efforts in order to succeed in gaining additional support.[49]

Deily warned against drawing too many conclusions from his finding of a close correlation between library expenditures and "general goodness," for too many known exceptions make any predictions based on such goodness uncertain. He added that a host of local traditions might be more significant in any particular city than the variables indicated in his study.[50]

---

[48] Robert H. Deily, "Public Library Expenditures in Cities of over 1,000,000 Population in Relation to Municipal expenditures and Economic Ability" (Ph.D. dissertation, University of Chicago, 1941), pp. 206-07.
[49] Ibid., pp. 206-209.
[50] Ibid., pp. 208.

He pointed out, almost in passing, that library service was closely related to library expenditure (+.771, higher than most other correlations that he found) and that circulation was the most reliable measure of service as compared to the two other measures of service used, book stock and registration.[51] Using a complex formula to measure library service, Flint Purdy found the same thing several years earlier.[52]

One of Deily's findings concerns the nature of municipal library support. Library appropriations averaged $.647 per capita, while library taxes averaged $.610 per capita, only a bit less than what the appropriations averaged. On the other hand, the $.610 represented 1.8 percent of total municipal effort, whereas the $.647 was only 1.4 percent. Deily concludes, and echoes Joechkel, that the measure-of-effort figure is a useful one for libraries supported by a special tax.[53]

Another finding was that in Southern cities, where the percentage of Negroes in the total population was high, both library support and services were low.[54] The study did not include findings relating Negro population, library support, and library service in Northern cities.

---

[51] Ibid., pp. 208.

[52] George Flint Pury, "Public Library Service in the Middle West," *Library Quarterly,* VIII, 3 (July 1938), p. 367.

[53] Deily, p. 279. He cites Carleton B. Joeckel, *Government of the American Public Library* (Chicago: University of Chicago Press, 1935), p. 220, which reports that as of 1930, appropriations yielded 1.3 percent of total municipal income, while special taxes yielded 2 percent.

[54] Ibid., p. 211.

Deily's final statement of findings is that cities with large total expenditures spend a reasonably high per capita amount for their library support, that "underprivileged" cities make a small effort, and that medium-sized, moderately well-off cities in the Midwest try hardest.[55] He observed that national minimum standards for library service probably could not be reached without some federal support, for regional variations in library strength and taxing power were too great, especially since the states and federal governments had siphoned off most of the most productive taxes.[56]

From these résumés of doctoral dissertation, it is clear that a substantial amount of attention has been devoted already to the impact of the depression on library services, but that no single comprehensive study has been undertaken. In addition, several areas remain unexplored. Herdman's work covered more of the field than either of the other two, but confined itself to the years 1930-1935 and to a limited range of statistics. Stanford restricted himself to a single federal program, and Deily directed his attention primarily to library support during the decade.

*Books, Articles, and Reports—1930-1940*

Among the earliest studies of the depression's effect on public libraries were those that treated general matters. Librarians were attempting to assess a situation that they only gradually came to realize was unparalleled in their experience. Many of their comments show they shared lack of prescience along with the nation's leaders, except

---

[55] Ibid.
[56] Ibid., p. 212.

for an early article written by Waples, Carnovsky, and Randall and a book by Robert L. Duffus[57], which made accurate comments on the depression's effects. Randall[58] had appeared in the bibliography of most subsequent works. It was a comprehensive study of the depression's effect on libraries from the beginning up to the date of the article's publication on October 1932. First, the authors found that budget cuts were averaging about 8 percent in all libraries for the twelve to fifteen months that libraries had really been subjected to the full force of the depression's impact, and that about two-thirds of all libraries had suffered budget cuts by mid-1932. During the same period, they found that book circulation had increased by a quarter to a third, indicating that as early as 1932, libraries were being forced to serve more with less.[59]

Salary budgets had not yet suffered substantially, the 15 percent cuts having been absorbed by the book account, with libraries severely reducing the number of new titles and copies they purchased. Larger libraries were able to save money by reducing the number of periodical subscriptions, while smaller libraries cut the binding budget for periodicals. All had eliminated commercial rebinding or curtailed either quantity or quality, or both.[60] Where salary budget had been reduced, the budgeting technique most often used had been allowing vacated positions to go unfilled. More painful moves were to follow.[61]

---

[57] Duffus.
[58] Waples, Carnovsky, and Randall.
[59] Ibid., pp. 324-26.
[60] Ibid., pp. 327-31.
[61] Ibid., p. 333.

Other early cuts that were widely used were elimination of special services, such as service to institutions, deposit stations and readers' advisers, and simplification of routines, such as those used in circulation.[62] The amounts of saving realized from these economies varied from one library size class to another, but overall substantial book budget reductions produced the largest savings, followed by small decreases in the salaries budget, and finally by economies from small-amount accounts such as building maintenance, binding, and periodicals.[63]

The authors suggested that librarians do a more effective job presenting their cases for stable budgets, that they master the art of forceful presentation, that they learn precisely whom they are serving, and with what, and in what quantity, for in the battle for municipal dollars they should not let those with figures that are easier to marshall outstrip them in claiming resources to equal their needs.[64]

At about the same time, in 1933, Duffus's extremely sympathetic popular work on libraries appeared. He showed how the public library was an indispensable agency in fighting the effects of the depression on the population.[65] Unfortunately, those who read the book lacked either the power, or the money, or the influence to generate money that would have provided for public libraries as Duffus indicated they should be supported. No libraries in the sample referred to his claim for libraries, nor to his generous descriptions of the libraries visited in

---

[62] Ibid., p. 335.
[63] Ibid., p. 336.
[64] Ibid., pp. 337-40.
[65] Duffus, pp. 1-4.

his research to gain information for chapters on the tribulations of specific libraries.

*State and Federal Aid*

Because the state and federal governments seemed to have the taxing power that municipalities lacked, directors of public libraries turned their attention to state and federal aid to supply the revenue they sorely needed. In doing so, they began the most heated debate the public library world experienced in the decade. Any recommendation was likely to provoke a retort, and the level of discourse varied as emotion conflicted with reason and fact.

The kind of federal aid studied by Stanford (discussed earlier in the dissertation section) caused little controversy. Neither librarians nor the public they served objected on theoretical grounds to participation in federally funded relief programs. Writings on federal programs usually accepted the results of relief-based programs but contested the wisdom of such federal subventions.

The projects carried on under the auspices of the Federal Emergency Relief Administration were surveyed in a 1934 report published in the American Library Association Bulletin.[69] Because the program was fairly new and the guidelines changed from time to time, the report began with a review of the rules under which FERA operated, merging it with a survey of the kinds of programs that libraries could operate under the FERA rules.[70] The

---

[69] Julia Wright Merrill, et. al., "Library Projects Under FERA," *American Library Association Bulletin*, XXVIII, 10, Part 2 (October 1934), pp. 823-39.
[70] Ibid., pp. 826-29.

CHAPTER TWO 37

bulk of the article covered numerous local efforts that had achieved a measure of success,[71] and ended with a review of the planned New York state project.[72] Some of the difficulties accompanying FERA programs are listed in Chapter I of this dissertation.[73] Briefly restated, since the programs were labor-intensive and could require the use of little additional capital, they usually had to be hastily planned and could not provide the internal coordination of elements. Thus they were, in a sense, opportunistic requiring the utilization of whatever was at hand. Some of these problems were reflected in the 1934 report.

One of the words introduced into the national consciousness by the New Deal was "planning." No program seemed complete without a cadre of planners and within a few months, the library profession also had a plan of its own. At its annual conference in Montreal in 1934, the American Library Association Council endorsed a plan that entailed federal aid for libraries and an assumption by the national government of responsibility for leadership of the library community, a nationwide program of state certification for librarians, state aid for school libraries, a network-like association among scholarly libraries to abet research efforts, and public library leagues designed to serve large numbers of people.[74] None of these proved so controversial among librarians that a second look at the concept was voted by the Executive Council. In fact, nothing further happened in national library planning for

---

[71] Ibid., pp. 829-38.
[72] Ibid., pp. 838-39.
[73] Ibid., pp. 16-17.
[74] "National Plan for Libraries," *Library Journal*, LIX (September 1, 1934), pp. 661-63.

another five years. When a revised plan appeared in 1938, the language concerned with federal aid remained but the responsibility of the federal government had changed from appropriating and administering grants to merely appropriating.[75] Administration of grants was to become the responsibility of appropriate state library agencies. The plan affirmed the American Library Association's belief that the support and government of public libraries were fundamentally a local matter, while leadership was the federal government's responsibility.[76]

Federal aid was not alone in creating policy difficulties for municipal libraries. The question of state aid elicited explanations but not the controversy created by federal aid. The primary purpose of state aid according to its proponents was to equalize service and to extend it to the otherwise unserved population. State aid was seen as a means to get the funds from the state general fund rather than from a special tax, to appropriate the funds as a part of the general appropriation bill rather than as a separate piece of legislation, and to administer it through the state library extension agency, if one existed.[77]

At about the same time that state aid policies were being developed, a special committee of the American Library Association was preparing its final report on federal aid. This extensive study, of which Carleton Joeckel was

---

[75] "National Plan for Libraries, as Revised and Adopted by the American Library Association Council, December 29, 1938," *American Library Association Bulletin*, XXXIII (February 1939), pp. 136-50.
[76] Ibid., pp. 145-46.
[77] "State Aid Policy Question," *American Library Association Bulletin*, XXX (September 1936), pp. 887-91.

the principal author, tried to answer the objections of opponents of federal aid. It reviewed the federal system of subventions and the major argument of both proponents and opponents of federal aid. It treated federal involvement in library service and concluded with recommendations for federal grants that even now are only partially realized.[78] Joeckel's appointment to chair the committee indicates something of the mood of the Association, for his sympathies in favor of federal aid had long been known.[79]

When, at length, the federal government turned its attention to the support of public libraries, support of all agencies of education in the country was under investigation by the President's Advisory Committee on Education, under the Chairman, Floyd Reeves. Joeckel, having already participated in preparing a lengthy report on federal aid for the American Library Association, was selected to do the staff study on libraries for the Committee. His second extended effort on federal aid paralleled the first in a number of important ways, not the least important being that federal aid was soundly endorsed.[80] Joeckel developed a complicated formula to determine the amount of federal aid that would be required to produce programs with funding variously at $1.00, $.75, and $.60 per capita, using an equalization approach that would

---

[78] American Library Association. Special Committee on Federal Aid, "Libraries and Federal Aid," *American Library Association Bulletin*, XXX, 5, Part 2 (May 1936), pp. 421-71.
[79] Carleton B. Joeckel, *Government of the American Public Library*, (Chicago: University of Chicago Press, 1935), p. 354.
[80] Joeckel, Library Service.

add whatever a municipality could not produce if taxing itself at a predetermined level to support library service.[81]

It was calculated that 1.93 percent of the average state taxing ability in the United States would be required to support library service for every citizen at a level of $1.00 per annum. According to the formula, any state whose taxing ability was such that 1.93 percent of the taxes it *could* collect did not reach $1.00 per capita would receive the deficit from federal aid. Other formulae were developed for $.75, using about 1.45 percent, and $.60, using 1.16 percent. Joeckel's focus was clearly on extending service to those without libraries, for in the formula he seemed to favor, he suggested about $17,000,000 in federal aid, with $9,300,000 of it reserved for equalization grants mostly for rural areas and rural states, $5,400,000 allocated on the basis of rural population, and the remainder, about 12 percent of the total, allotted on a percentage-of-present-expenditure basis.[82]

The issue of federal control was skirted somewhat by the statement that responsibility would be shared with the states. Joeckel indicated that federal-states cooperation in program development would take place within federal guidelines for library extension, and that federal audits would determine the proper administration of state and local programs. Beyond that, there would be no federal control.[83]

The controversy was partially and temporarily resolved when the Harrison-Fletcher-Thomas Bill to implement the Reeves Committee's recommendations was allowed to

---

[81] Ibid., pp.79-88.
[82] Ibid., p. 85.
[83] Ibid., pp. 88-89.

die in committee in 1938. Federal aid did not become a reality until the enactment in 1956 of the Library Service Act, which began federal involvement in library service, this time without much controversy.

*Library Unionization*

Unions for library personnel were the subjects for discussion among librarians during the latter part of the decade. The union movement had begun haltingly during the depression, with the National Industrial Recovery Act encouraging unions, but being invalidated, and with the National Labor Relations Act legalizing them but being tied up in litigation until 1938. The library debate on the issue is best summarized in two articles that appeared in the last third of the decade.

The earlier of the two articles was in two parts, a pro and a con. The stand opposed to library unions claimed that librarians did not seek a share of any profits as did industrial unionists, for unions were beneath the professional dignity of librarians, and that much of the activity of unions was for the aggrandizement of union leaders. Proponents of library unions attempted to refute those arguments and added that while librarians might forego striking, unions alone could guarantee their salaries and tenure.[84]

The issue was much debated. Bernard Berelson's article "Library Unionization" was the least polemic in

---

[84] "Should Librarians Unionize?" *Library Journal*, LXII (August 1937), pp. 587-93.

tone.⁸⁵ Berelson proceeded in scholarly fashion to trace labor's long history of support for education, suggesting that affiliation with labor might enable public librarians to draw library needs directly to labor's attention.⁸⁶ Berelson pointed out that although many American professions had unions, Americans were actually behind European countries in developing them.⁸⁷ He said that strikes, picketing and mass action had been foresworn in favor of negotiation, publicity, petitioning, and promotion of legislation;⁸⁸ he surveyed the five public libraries (Butte, Cleveland, Milwaukee, Chicago, and Grand Rapids) and the Library of Congress which were the only libraries with unions in the United States and showed their activities and levels of success.⁸⁹ Finally, he discussed the reasons usually advanced for the formation of unions.⁹⁰ Two important facts emerge about the article: 1) it did not attempt to refute pro-union statements made by union proponents nor to provide any information on the negative side of the controversy, and 2) it attracted no letters to the editors of library periodicals from public librarians in the sample. At any rate, unions for library employees were proposed and opposed by librarians. Library unions kept growing, slowly but steadily, but no other articles appeared in library periodicals to record further progress during the decade 1930-1940.

---

[85] Bernard Berelson, "Library Unionization," *Library Quarterly,* IX (October 1939), pp. 477-510.
[86] Ibid., pp. 479-83.
[87] Ibid., pp. 483-89.
[88] Ibid., pp. 488.
[89] Ibid., pp. 490-504.
[90] Ibid., pp. 505-10.

CHAPTER TWO 43

*Services*

The studies of library services during the depression were perhaps more numerous than studies of any other phase of library activity. Books, articles, and reports to a variety of government agencies reflected the growing attention to the people's access to and use of libraries. Many of these focused on the library's activities in depression times.

The first such article appeared early, following a day-long meeting of the American Library Executive Board at Forest Hills, Long Island on November 8, 1931. The article's thesis was that librarians then, more than at any previous time, were responsible for providing the community with material on the causes of the depression, on vocational readjustment, on trades and occupations, on family budgeting, and on homelife.[91] In addition, the library had to aid in maintaining morale for the host of unemployed who were turning to the library, people who needed the best and latest material on subjects of vital interest. The article suggested that libraries relate their efforts to those on the radio on similar subjects, using print material to amplify what potential readers would have heard over the air.[92] At the end of the article was a suggested list of materials—books, pamphlets, and magazine articles—on the unemployment problem, on leisure, and on Russia and the five-year plan. The latter indicated the extent of the interest Russia had generated early in the depression.[93]

---

[91] "Public Library and the Depression," *Wilson Bulletin for Librarians,* VI, 4 (December 1931), pp. 267-70.
[92] Ibid., p. 268.
[93] Ibid., 268-70.

William Converse Haygood, a student of the Graduate Library School of the University of Chicago, studied use of the New York Public Library and later reported in *Who Uses the Library.*[94] During the period of the one week in January, 1936 that Haygood studied, 20,000 people used one or more divisions of the Reference Department or one of the branches of the library and filled in his questionaires.[95] Haygood found that the public library was the prime book source of three quarters of the people who used it, and that another fifteen percent of his sample used academic libraries as their prime source. Thus, in January 1936, nine library users in ten used the library more than they used any other book-supplying agency.[96] Certain other findings were useful: users with more education placed heavier burdens on the library, but succeeded better in adapting what they found to their needs.[97]

A major effort that acknowledged indebtedness to Haygood's work was the *Geography of Reading*, a study undertaken by Louis Round Wilson, Dean of the Graduate Library School of the University of Chicago and President of the American Library Association in 1934-1935, which amassed more information than any other book

---

[94] William Converse Haygood, *Who Uses the Public Library; A Survey of the Patrons of the Circulation and Reference Departments of the New York Public Library*. (Chicago: University of Chicago Press, 1938).
[95] Ibid., p. 123.
[96] Ibid., p. 115.
[97] Ibid., p. 113.

treated in this chapter.[98] Wilson made a comprehensive survey of the location of public library strength throughout the United States, synthesizing previous research done on the location and strength of the nation's libraries. He studied the aspects of geography, population, and economic development that he considered contributed to the strength of the libraries and to the growth of bookstores, rental libraries, and subscriptions to magazines. He also related these aspects to the growth of public schools and agencies for adult education and to the growth of communication facilities. So ambitious an understanding could not be uniformly successful. Thus, after more than four hundred pages of text, charts, maps, and footnotes, Wilson produced a series of recommendations, the first of which was that there be more study,[99] at a time when most librarians were requesting direction, not observation.

Wilson recommended statistical studies, more books for the semi-literate, more planning, laws to effectuate the plans, extension of service to the rural areas, library education in the schools, more interlibrary loan and other services to scholars (based on the card, bibliographical and interlibrary loan services of the Library of Congress), the assumption by the states of responsibility for library service so as to achieve equality of service for all, and new inspiration for the librarians of America.[100] One could not quarrel with Wilson's recommendations. The liberal wing

---

[98] Louis Round Wilson, *Geography of Reading: A Study of the Status and Distribution of Libraries in the United States.* (Chicago: American Library Association and the University of Chicago, 1938).
[99] Ibid., p. 438.
[100] Ibid., pp. 438-42.

of the profession had endorsed them; the conservative wing would do so eventually. But as conclusions, they seemed to indicate that Wilson had labored strenuously to produce what most of the profession had already considered. The value and bulk of evidence that he assembled, however, made *The Geography of Reading*, a major work on libraries.

*Adult Education*

In the last third of the decade, many survey books on adult education appeared. The American Library Association's Adult Education Specialist John Chancellor wrote *Printed Page*,[101] which considered all aspects of a successful adult education program, including some material on the nascent science of readability. The last portion of the brochure was a survey of successful practices in several functioning programs. Chancellor was to be represented often in the bibliography of adult education. In the same year that he published *Printed Page*, he also wrote a study of the Library in the TVA Adult Education Program,[102] describing an interesting and replicable program. There was nothing particularly unique to the Tennessee Valley Authority that made a library program that succeeded with it unlikely to succeed elsewhere. One finding that supported current doctrine was that service must be nearby to the people who use it, for service that was re-

---

[101] John Chancellor, *Printed Page and the Public Platform,* Bulletin 1937, No. 27 (Washington: United States Office of Education 1937).
[102] John Chancellor, *Library in the TVA Adult Education Program* (Chicago: American Library Association, 1937).

mote, no matter how efficient or needed would not be used.[103]

Two 1938 books on adult education are interesting when set side by side. *Adult Education*,[104] a study by Floyd Reeves, Professor of Education at the University of Chicago, was criticized because its author asked too much of libraries for adult education. Reeves, in surveying the practice of adult education in New York State, described it as largely a classroom or club room effort, pacing demands on the leader to teach and not asking enough of the advisory service offered by many libraries. In *Public Library—A People's University*, Johnson placed responsibility for leadership in adult education squarely on librarians. He said that only their natural reticence could inhibit their functioning in a leadership role.[106] Librarians tended to accept the charge that they become leaders in adult education, but some librarians were reluctant to assume this role for they felt that they had stronger and more pressing duties. The term "the people's university" for the public library, however, captured the sentiment of librarians about the proper function of their libraries and the phrase has endured.

A voluminous study on adult education was edited by Chancellor,[107] who surveyed successful adult education programs everywhere. This interesting volume was a series of very short articles, each by a successful adult edu-

---

[103] Ibid., p. 59.
[104] F. W. Reeves, *Adult Education* (New York: McGray-Hill, 1938).
[106] Ibid., p. 73.
[107] John Chancellor, ed., *Helping Adults to Learn: the Library in Action* (Chicago: American Library Association, 1939).

cator-librarian describing the solution of adult education programs or describing the outstanding elements of a successful program. Only the last forty-four pages, in which Chancellor tried to synthesize the preceding two hundred, offered systematic treatment of adult education programs. The book was useful. It contained sound information, but too few people reviewed it. It was not even covered by the *Book Review Digest.*

Jennie Flexner's excellent *Readers' Advisers at Work*[108] is a study of the twelve-year history of her service at New York Public Library, together with enough presentation of human situations that any reader and potential readers' adviser could not miss the point that the patrons of such service are humans, not case studies; that they have problems they wish to solve, not bundles of data to be assessed; and that the approach of the adviser is important in the success of the patron in finding the material needed.[109]

*Conclusion*

These, then, were some of the materials on the matters that were of greatest concern to the public library profession during the period of the depression, 1930-1940. They have ranged from administrative problems, such as worry about depression impact and finances, to newly emerging problems and programs like the potential effect of federal and state aid, to concern for what the library does, for whom, and why, and adult education. Some of

---

[108] Jennie M. Flexner and Bryon C. Hopkings, *Readers' Advisers at Work: A Survey of Development in New York Public Library* (New York: American Association for Adult Education, 1941).
[109] Ibid., 72-73.

these concerns were peculiar to the depression. Others are still with us. Pensions for library employees are now taken for granted. So is state aid. Federal aid has never been a certain source of revenue, especially a continuing source. But no major objections are heard from librarians when federal appropriations for support of library services are debated.

On the other hand, we are still concerned with services. Burgeoning demands for information, for escape reading, and for material in formats that were only experimental in the period of the depression have added to the administrative burdens of the successors of the directors whose writings were analyzed in this study. And finally, money, the great problem of the depression, is demonstrably always a problem in libraries whether the economy is depressed or expanding. Until dollars can be generated spontaneously, we shall have articles devoted to budget problems of libraries.

## Chapter 3
## Methodology

*Introduction*

Bernard R. Berelson, author of *Content Analysis in Communications Research* and one of the pioneers of content analysis, gives the definition that has become a standard: "Content analysis, is a research technique for the objective, systematic, and quantitative description of the manifest content of communication."[110] Paraphrasing Berelson, Griggs notes that in content analysis "emphasis and first focus are upon the content itself, it employs a formal and systematic definition of categories, and it breaks down complex themes into components."[111] Since inception, content analysis has been used as a research tool for propaganda analysis, analysis of newspaper communication coverage of economic conditions during a recession in 1957-58,[112] analysis of radio broadcasts,[113] analysis of

---

[110] Bernard R. Berelson, *Content Analysis in Communications Research* (Glencoe, Illinois: Free Press, 1952), p. 18.
[111] Harry R. Griggs, "Coverage of National Economic Conditions by Five Mass Circulation Daily Newspaper during Three Crucial Months of the 1957-58 Recession" (Ph.D. dissertation, States University of Iowa, 1962), p. 52.
[112] Ibid.
[113] David Wakefield Shepard, "An Experiment in Content Analysis: the Radio Addresses of Henry J. Taylor: 1945-1950" (Ph.D. dissertation, University of Minnesota, 1953).

speeches made accepting presidential nominations,[114] and analysis of newspaper treatment of the Kerr-Mills Bill to provide medical care for the elderly.[115] Recent developments in the use of content analysis have linked it with computer techniques and with sophisticated linguistics, psychological, and computer concepts.[116]

The writer's decision to use content analysis in this study was prompted by the desire to produce a bias-free study of the effects of the depression on American public libraries. It was believed that the technique, with its requisites of a carefully defined universe, meticulously selected categories, pretested coding form, and strict rules of procedure, would be an effective bar to conscious or unconscious investigator prejudice and thereby guarantee objective results. The Committee that directed this study supplied invaluable aid and advice in avoiding the problems that the unwary may encounter in the course of research.

Content analysis technique requires the researcher to determine the limits of his universe and to produce a list of categories, a coding form, and a procedure to be used consistently. Once the universe is established, each phase of the production of category, coding form, and procedure is tested against a sample body of journal articles that are subject-related but outside the universe. Correc-

---

[114] Philip J Stone, et. al., *The General Inquirer; A Computer Approach to Content Analysis,* (Cambridge, Massachusetts: M.I.T. Press, 1967), pp. 359-400.

[115] Robert Lewis Donohew, "Publisher Attitude and Community Conditions as Factors in Newspaper Coverage of a Social Welfare Issue" (Ph.D. dissertation, State University of Iowa, 1965).

[116] Stone, pp. 2-279.

tions are then made on the categories, coding form, and procedure before the actual analysis of the universe is undertaken.

*Universe*

The universe is the all-inclusive body of pre-defined material on which content analysis is to be applied. In this study, the universe was composed of the depression-related writings in annual reports and journal articles of the directors of public libraries serving populations of 200,000 and over on census day, 1 April, 1930.

A number of considerations dictated that choice. First, the public library directors serving the largest public libraries would be representative of the librarians who have had to deal with depression problems and would be most representative of the interest of the public they served during the depression period. Second, the population base of 200,000 and over was the largest recognized size class of libraries for which the *American Library Association Bulletin* published annual statistics during the decade. And third, the directors of the largest public libraries would be recognized and respected members of the library profession whose views would command respect and attention from both their colleagues and the public.

The decision to use writings in annual reports and journals was made in an effort to include those forms in which a large number of librarians in the aggregate had written. Annual reports from the library directors over the depression decade constituted a regular source of writing that would presumably show what the directors were most concerned about. However, producing the annual report was a local matter for each library. In some libraries, each annual report was a volume running to over a hundred pages; in others, the report consisted of a few pages stapled together.

A few libraries in the universe had no annual reports at all. Journal articles were used because they would be most likely to contain the views of the library directors about issues, problems, and concerns which they wanted to bring to the attention of the profession, and it was extremely probable that the journals would publish any materials that this group of library directors would offer for publication. Books were ruled out of the universe because too few were produced during the thirties and representation in them was too uneven.

Thus, the universe, as defined, was the one best constituted to provide the body of content that had all categories to which the directors turned their attention. The authors selected were those to whom the rest of the profession were most likely to pay attention, and the forms were those in which a maximum number of authors were likely to have written. No other universe could have met the requirements as well.

*Categories*

A category is a simple, single unit of idea into which the material in the universe can be broken down. Berelson said of content analysis that it "stands or falls by its categories."[117] Richard W. Budd added that categories "must accurately, fit the needs of the study so that they answer the question originally asked, be exhaustive (relative to the

---

[117] Berelson, p. 147.

problem), and be mutually exclusive."[118] For these reasons, the formulation of the list of categories received very careful attention.

The formulation was carried out in a series of steps, the first of which was to identify in *Library Literature* and read everything that had been written about libraries in the depression, to determine (1) whether it introduced material that the researcher had not previously encountered or (2) whether it set out to summarize a large body of previously published material. From these readings, every possible topic treated that might in any way be depression-related was listed as a category. The collection of topics thus obtained became the preliminary list of categories.

A random selection of the 632 depression-related articles found in the search of *Library Literature* was then made and analyzed, using the preliminary list of categories. It was found that a desirable step would be to merge some categories that were so nearly synonymous as to be indistinguishable for coding purposes. In fact, certain authors to discuss ideas designated by other categories, as for example, adult education and readers' advisory service, used some of the words designating preliminary categories. Merging such categories simplified the task of recording without reducing the accuracy of the result. At the same time, the coding form on which the recording was being done was examined for suitability.

After the category list had been improved, a second random selection of articles was made and the list refined still further. It was found that certain terms used for cate-

---

[118] Richard W. Budd, Robert K. Thorp, and Lewis Donohew, *Content Analysis of Communications* (New York: Macmillan Company, 1967), p. 39.

gories were misleading in that they used words current in the thirties that had since been replaced by other words. For example, "conscience weeks" in the depression became "fine cancellation" on the list.

The terms were clustered around six major headings: (1) library buildings, procedures, and techniques; (2) the economic situation; (3) books and bibliography; (4) relations with the public; (5) new relations with the government; and (6) personnel. The relation between library personnel and other professional concerns of directors was perceived and the two groups of categories were merged. Thereafter, the committee suggested that there were, in effect, three groups: (1) those dealing with the library as an institution (including library buildings, procedures, and techniques and books and bibliography, (2) the library in its socio-political context (including relations with the public and new relations with government), and (3) the economic situation. The reduction to three in the number of groups greatly simplified dealing with the results of Chapters IV and V, in addition to substantially increasing the logic of the groupings.

*The Coding Form*

The coding form is the form on which every bit of collected data is recorded. At first, it seemed a prosaic item, merely needed for record keeping. Such was not the case, for the coding form ultimately had to be able to house all the information that analysis would require. It was recognized that the coding form would need to show for the article it encoded bibliographic information to the following extent: the author, the article, the type of article, how the article related to the objectives of the dissertation, how the author treated the information, the category, and enough brief information to identify the content. Several forms were developed and discarded. The initial effort was too simple, providing only coded bibliographic information and a coded indication of the category of the article. Technically, these were all that the researcher's purpose required in the study, but for any information concerning the article other than the coded category, the researcher needed to return to the article itself; the need showed a deficiency in the coding form.

The next attempt at the coding form tried to provide for every possible combination of approaches that an author might make to his information. It was over-ambitious, and hence space-wasting, for no article supplied more than a third of what it asked.

After numerous problems arose from attempts to show inter-relationships between encoded materials on the same coding form, it was decided to encode each category separately on a copy of the form. The presence of information related to another category would have to be shown on another form, and the effort to show a relation between categories abandoned.

The first, overly-simple coding form was never used. The forms used in the two trials with materials outside the universe were the second described above and another that tried to simplify it. Both of them contributed to the development of the form that was finally used.[119] That form met the twin tests of providing space for desired information and of not requiring material that only occasional items from the universe might supply.

---

[119] See Appendix IIB, pp. 175-81.

*Procedure*

Once the tasks of defining the universe, selecting the categories, and developing the coding form had been accomplished, encoding the data was largely a repetitive activity. Each item in the universe was read paragraph by paragraph, and content of the paragraph that fitted into one of the categories was encoded for it.

The major problem in the coding phase was coping with the ennui that may prevent consistency in handling the material at hand. No investigator has offered a means for dealing with the problem, though most of them have mentioned it. This investigator partially solved it by setting up a series of goals: an author completed, a library's annual report completed, or whatever might serve to provide an intermediate sense of accomplishment. It worked reasonably well.

Once all coding was completed, the data were, for purposes of convenience, keypunched into eighty-column tabulator cards. The computer was not used in the coding or in the analysis of the data, except for the purposes of sorting and counting. For those operations, it was a welcome saver of time, and amply justified the effort that had gone into keypunching. The cards, when punched, could be sorted by author, by date, by category, or by one within another, and the results of the sort counted mechanically. The elimination of error was helpful in this stage.

Finally, once all of the keypunching had been completed and checked for accuracy, the sorting was done and the counts were made. Those counts, and the data that accompanied them, served as the basis for the content of Chapters IV and V.

A difficulty arose when Chapters IV and V were being drafted: there were too few synonyms for citations and allusions. Therefore, the word "mentions" was used. The term "discussions" was reserved, however, for those instances where the directors' comments were relevant to the data encoded in columns 15-17 of the tabulator card. The areas concerned with director concern about operations, services, and policies. The expressions of concern in these three areas were frequently more detailed, so the term was most appropriately used here.

*Summary*

The use of content analysis laces numerous tasks on the researcher in the selection of the universe, in the preparation of the list of categories, in the development of the coding form, and in the refinement of the procedure. The rigors of the technique require that each phase be done perfectly, for incomplete or imperfect handling of each phase immediately shows itself in even more problems that demand immediate attention and solution before the next step can proceed. Thus, the researcher is constantly being checked by the method into rethinking his problems, objectives, and procedures. Once the whole process has been carried through, with the categories and the coding form perfectly determined so that they could contain the data necessary to the analysis, the procedure of coding goes smoothly. At the end of the coding, when all the data are marshaled into quantitative numbers, the researcher can analyze the results, and the objectivity of the numbers he is faced with gives him the assurance that no hidden inclinations on his part affected the results of his research. Thus, content analysis fulfills its definition as a research technique that provides an objective means of analyzing the data of content.

*Chapter 4*
Findings Based on Content Analysis

*Introduction*

The analysis of the findings of this dissertation required knowledge of the historical background, presented in Chapter One, library background in Chapter Two, and technical background in Chapter Three. This chapter attempts to describe the categories from a number of viewpoints and to make some comments about the library directors whose writings comprise the universe.

Initial attention to the categories will attempt to answer these questions:

1. Which of the categories received the most attention?
2. In which journals did they receive the most attention?
3. Which received decade-long attention?
4. Which received sporadic attention?
5. When did they receive sporadic attention?

Using the paragraph as the coding unit required of the researcher that he ignore potentially interesting data that were not related to the coded subject of the paragraph. The advantage of the definition was that it kept the body of data manageable; the disadvantage was that it eliminated from consideration some possibly useful data.

*Source of Comments*

Approximately seventy-five percent of the total comments encoded as parts of the universe came from annual reports; the remaining twenty-five percent came from articles. Comments in annual reports, therefore, constituted seventy-five percent of all attention paid to all categories. The total universe consisted of approximately 3,800 pages of annual reports and about 620 pages of articles.

A problem with the annual reports, as with nearly all official statements, was that they tended to avoid discussing controversial matters. The articles provide adequate testimony of the disagreements that occurred during the depression. Written evidence seems to indicate that all the controversies were among librarians, that boards never became involved. However, hints in some articles tend to negate that evidence, but no librarian used his annual reports to disagree with a position taken by the board to which he reported.

*Categories Receiving Major Attention*

The categories about which the library directors wrote most frequently during the period 1930-40 were: 1) contributions of relief agencies to the running of libraries, 2) demand for books, 3) demand for services, 4) adult education, 5) patron reading interests, and 6) budget. The first and last of these were of paramount and immediate concern; the depression triggered the formation of public agencies to provide jobs for the otherwise unemployed, and budgets became even more of a problem than usual during this period of economic contraction. Heightened interest in the other categories is also understandable. Book circulation, as Herdman showed,[120] increased dramatically during the first years of the depression, as did the demand for other library services. Reading interests also changed during the period as library patrons tried first to escape from the reality of the depression and then to understand and cope with that reality. One of the efforts that libraries maintained, improved, and expanded during the period, at a time when other library programs were failing for lack of support, was the adult education program, which had been accorded widespread formal recognition for only about a decade when the depression began.

*Relief Agency Contributions*

Discussions of the contributions of relief agencies to the libraries of the sample took place largely after the establishment of New Deal programs in 1933. The few mentions of the small state and local work relief programs were insignificant portions of the universe. Those workers hired by the Civil Works Administration (CWA), the Federal Emergency Relief Administration (FERA), the National Youth Administration (NYA), and the Works Progress Administration (WPA) in the main discharged routine clerical and maintenance tasks such as filing, cleaning books and buildings, mending books, repairing building and their areas, and painting exteriors and interiors.

A number of projects, however, fell outside normal library routines. In Philadelphia and to a lesser extent in New York, the library WPA workers included some who

---

[120] Herdman, p. 7.

were hired to copy manuscripts of unpublished music. The Free Library of Philadelphia specialized in the works of composers from the United States, especially contemporary people (R154, R155, R156).[121] Much bibliographic work was not routine: Louis Bailey of Queens reported the copying and indexing of Long Island manuscripts that would otherwise not have been available to scholars (R209). Carl Roden reported that the WPA and the Chicago Public Library cooperated on classes for adults, and on another project to film and index Chicago newspapers (R57, R58, R59). Milton Lord reported that at the Boston Public Library, the WPA workers helped in a number of catalog projects, one being to recoup cards on new three by five inch stock, another to remaking the shelf list, which had been in folio volumes, and a third being to recatalog all of the scholarly books in the collection (R21, R22, R23, R24, R25).

From Akron, Will Collins reported mixed success: CWA people indexed play collections efficiently in 1934 but in 1937, the WPA workers cost an average of nine and one half cents a copy to trim and mount pictures, a job that library personnel handled for two cents each (R2, R5). William Hamilton from Dayton, Beatrice Winser from Newark, and Malcolm Wyer from Denver each reported success in work on regional union catalogs (R74, R146, J203).

---

[121] "R" and "J" enclosed in parenthesis refer to the primary sources of the universe. An article reference is designated by "J" and the number of the article; see Appendix I-D, pp.160-172. An annual report reference is designated by "R" and the number of the annual report; see Appendix I-C, pp. 152-159.

CHAPTER FOUR 65

Milton Ferguson from Brooklyn and Harry Miller Lydenberg of New York discussed extensive branch enlargement projects handled by the CWA and WPA (R32, R35, R135, R13*). George Bowerman reported the rewiring of buildings under the auspices of the PWA and CWA in 1934 (R248). Reports stated that the work performance was adequate provided there were sufficient direction and supervision.

*Demand for Books*

Early in the decade, discussions of the demand for books conformed nearly always to one pattern and then to a slightly different one later. For the first two years, directors said that the increased clientele, together with a severely decreased book fund, would quickly exhaust the collection (R29, R58, R71, R130, R195). Toward the middle of the period, comments tended to indicate that collections were pretty well worn out, and, on occasion, employees were similarly exhausted. (R11, R33, R134, R175, R176, R227).

During the last three years of the decade, what comments there were (and these decreased dramatically after demand ceased to be so great a problem) indicated that circulation was decreasing as people were returning to work, that book funds were increasing, and that circulation of fiction had decreased the most (R70, R128, R138, R202, R221).

In 1930, Clarence Sherman reported that unemployment was sending more men to the library than had used it previously, and that more children were using it also, but not more women (R193). Carl Roden was the first to report a decrease in circulation: the Chicago Public Library during 1929 and 1930 had some of the earliest difficulties with taxation, a result of which was the reduction by one-third of the service hours of the branches. Circulation dropped about four percent (R57). The following year, when the branches returned to full schedules, book circulation had fallen distressingly, the depleted bookstock, which had decreased 30 percent, was blamed (R60).

In that same year, 1933, which some of the historians called the worst year of the depression, Sherman stated that libraries and the reading of good books would continue and that librarians would be needed to serve the readers (R196). During the time when most directors were complaining of the inadequacy of resources, Sherman's optimism was not generally shared. Ralph Munn pointed out that the Pittsburgh Carnegie Library's books and staff was exhausted in 1935, and when the recession of 1937 caused circulation to increase again, the library resources were additionally hard pressed (R176, R178).

Some comments about circulation were not related to the depression. In 1937, Will Collins reported that a strike in Akron had caused a large increase, and Beatrice Winser warned that librarians could control fiction/nonfiction percentages of circulation by controlling purchases (R5, J198). She added that the library's responsibility was to select the material to be purchased, not to delegate the selection to those who otherwise would patronize the rental libraries and other purveyors of cheap reading material.

CHAPTER FOUR 67

*Demand for Services*

Demand for services other than the loan of books followed a pattern similar to that of book circulation during the decade (R151, R193, R210). As early as 1930, many libraries reported that demand for reference service had increased dramatically. As the period progressed, limitations on the ability to buy new materials and the ability to use them when bought (available staff was occupied with answering questions in the shortest possible time, usually by the expedient method of directing the questioner to the card catalog) resulted in decreases in the amount of service that was reported (R28, R132, R133, R134, R196, R241, J159). Comments about the quality of the service indicated that the employees continued to try to provide service—references, reserve, renewal—although they had limited resources with which to do so.

An early statement on the cost, long term, of the increased demand came from Ralph Munn of Pittsburgh, who said that the reference department staff was devoted entirely to answering questions, that its concern for the development of specialized material—clipping files and the like—had to be overlooked (R171). Clarence Sherman reported in that same year that patron registration had increased until one-third of the population of Providence was registered (R193). Anne Mulheron reported that even fines for overdue books had increased (R183). In contrast, most librarians said, as hard time continued, that borrowers were becoming more and more careful to return their borrowed books on time. The following year, Mulheron said that the Portland Public Library staff had begun objecting to the conditions that required of them that they provide service without the means to make that service good. (R184).

In 1932, Milton Ferguson argued that the attempt to answer all of the needs of all the people, irrespective of the quality of those needs, precluded giving adequate attention to any of them (J90). In 1933, David Cadugan reported from the Pittsburgh Allegheny Library that, despite decreases in the services it could offer, the new users had not deserted the library (R163). Will Collins, writing in the Akron Public Library's annual report, said that although many people had been forced to give up personal telephones, the library's telephone work had increased (R1). He added that while often the questions from patrons were vague, the answers were expected to be specific.

In 1934, George Bowerman said that despite book and staff budget decreases, patrons were making heavy use of the District of Columbia Public Library (R248). David Cadugan continued to repot that the new users were still faithful to the library (R164). Linda Eastman, in 1934, attributed to an improving economy the fact that the users were more serious and that the newspaper room was the haven of fewer who simply sat, trying to keep warm (R65). Both Bowerman and Harry Miller Lydenberg of the New York Public Library reported special provisions for crossword puzzle contestants—a peculiarity of the decade—who would have crowded all users except themselves from the library (R133, R248).

In 1937, Clarence Sherman said that the use of the reference service had grown throughout the decade (R200). In the main, directors merely cited the year's statistics and either claimed that increasing budgets made more service possible, or said that increasing employment reduced the service demand. The latter, as was indicated earlier, formed the majority.

*Adult Education*

Approximately one-fourth of the librarians in the sample commented on adult education during the decade, many of them doing so frequently. At a time when budgets were being reduced generally, they found money to inaugurate programs in this new area of library service. Their comments show a wide-ranging concept of adult education, one that could comprehend a program that had nothing more than a readers' adviser to others that included preparation of reading lists developed around the needs, interests, and abilities of the individual requester (R171, R131, J71). Other libraries, working with agencies such as the American Association for Adult Education, attempted to offer classes for Negroes, the foreign-born, and those seeking to change vocations or to understand the economic conditions that necessitated the attempt to change (J7, J15, R53, R137). In 1932, Linda Eastman devoted extensive comment to the subject, claiming that, first, adult education in the depression had become largely vocational education and that to do an acceptable job in such work, librarians had to have new materials (J71). Some indexes, she continued, and the material to accompany them could be prepared with a minimum of cost. She stressed that two problems could not be overlooked: librarians should not forget the important task of educating the whole person seeking advice. Merely to add to vocational skills, even to upgrade employability, was to fail to fulfill a major responsibility.

Adam Strohm rejected the idea of a program built around a designated readers' adviser or specifically called adult education (R85). Other librarians did not accept his contention that the entire staff bore responsibility for the education of the citizen and that such education was the major purpose of the library, although he persevered in stating it.

In 1935, Lydenberg suggested that the patrons of adult education service at New York Library seemed to have turned from economic-related interests to general cultural concerns; he regretted that often when the readers' advisory service sent patrons to their branches for specific books, those books were unavailable there (R134). Finally, Chalmers Hadley pointed out that many of the users of adult education programs were uneducated and many of the books lent to them were beyond their reading abilities (J94). He recommended providing for those people, for their adult-education-related interests, material that they could understand.

At the end of the decade, no final comments on depression-related adult education were made by any of the directors in the sample. They turned from the depression, to culture, to war. And, as it happened in the newspapers and history books, the change was not an abrupt break but rather an imperceptible gradation.

*Reading Interest Areas*

Comments on the reading interests of library borrowers during the depression, to the extent that they were not predictable, have already been indicated. To restate: early in the period, many readers wanted simply to escape from the economic, social, and psychological problems that they could neither cope with nor understand. As time passed, they began concurrent efforts to understand the problems and to cope with them. These concerns continued as the depression progressed; interest in fiction decreased throughout the decade while interest in learning grew. Fiction purchases decreased in many libraries (J52, J132, R177). The last few years saw a turn from unspecific requests and interests to new ones related to the coming war (R69, R137).

Generalizations about reading interests should not be overvalued. Decreases in fiction as a portion of total borrowings were measured in a few percentage points, and gains in non-fiction areas were similarly small. But it was upon small increases, amounting to a percent or two, that the directors in the sample commented—and that they found significant.

*Budget*

Depression problems were reflected, logically enough, in budget reductions. Libraries were relatively untouched during the first two years, when they could spend their accumulated surpluses, if any, or the tax money that was still available to them because of lags between tax collections and the beginnings of fiscal years. But as these sources of funds grew less abundant, concerns with finance increased.

Budget was a matter for serious treatment during the time when revenues and expenditures were at their lowest, but during the first three years of the depression, concern was relatively minimal. Thereafter, the level of concern increased and held at the raised level until the effect of New Deal programs permeated the economy. Then, in

1938, 1939, and 1940, interest in budget matters decreased considerably.

In Seattle, Judson Jennings reported a major cut in his 1930 budget, atypically, but at the same time said that for the following year more money would be available (R223). The report of the following year indicated the poor quality of Jenning's prophecy, and he was not alone in being hurt in 1932 (R224, R225)

Adam Strohm and Edwin Anderson made conflicting reports: Strohm said that the Detroit Public Library's budget especially for books, could not tolerate the strain being placed on it (R81), while Anderson did not think that the New York Public Library Reference Division had suffered as a result of the depression in 1931 (R130). Paul North Rice was an early commentator on the specific problem that the depression posed for municipalities: tax delinquencies had severely cut into the budget of the Dayton Library (R71, R72). Budgets had started down because, as Harold Brigham reported from Louisville, taxes to support the budgets could not be collected and endowments were not as lucrative as they have been (J24).

Because the Chicago Public Library encountered special problems with the collection of its taxes, Carl Roden reported unusual difficulties: as early as May 1931, book buying stopped and after October, salaries went unpaid (J152). The staff was reduced twenty percent, and branch hours were cut. And for Chicago, as for elsewhere, budget problems still had several years to run.

From Providence, Rhode Island, Clarence Sherman reported that the Providence Public Library's endowments had protected it from the vagaries of the 1932 tax situation (R195). A year later, he claimed that the city ought to pay a larger share of the library's support (R196).

In 1935, he complained that the library's appropriation had not changed in ten years while service had increased fifty percent and the books were worn out (R198). Finally, in 1938, he said that in view of the mounting deficits in the library budget, the city would have to deal more fairly with its library (R201).

By the end of 1933, Judson Jennings had reported cuts totaling forty-four percent of the Seattle Public Library budget (R226). In 1932, between the Buffalo Public Library's budget approval and the beginning of the fiscal year, tax delinquencies forced the trimming of seventeen percent ($70,000) from an already trimmed budget (R40). Ralph Munn had to violate one of his own principles— not to cut the book budget—when in November 1931, he was given five hours to cut eight percent, amounting to $46,000, from the Pittsburgh Carnegie Library budget (J133, R173).

In 1931, Gratia Countryman turned over to the Minneapolis Public Library staff the problem of making some of the decisions. The staff proposed eliminating: 1) references in the patron registration process, 2) book reserves, 3) overdue book notices from branches, 4) the keeping of elaborate, but unexplained statistical records, 5) annual inventories, printed annual reports, printed new book lists, and 6) evening hours during the summer, except on Mondays (J59).

During the next few years, comments about budget continued to indicate which budget items had been cut, how badly the library had been hurt by the cut, and how long recovery would require. New York Public Library provided interesting data. In the general cutbacks, the branches were among the first to be put on shortened hours, but because of the nature of the contract in New

York, however, those built with Carnegie money were protected and could not be so treated. So while the rest of the system went on short hours, the six Carnegie branches maintained full services (R133, R137, R138).

In 1935, Jennings still had to report that the Seattle budget was painfully low (R228). While other libraries had mentioned partial restorations, his report talked of continued operation at less than sixty percent of earlier budget levels. In 1936, Harry Miller Lydenberg said that the 1936 materials budget of $80,000 was one third of what the library had for books, periodicals, and binding in 1932, and was inadequate for even the binding bill (R135).

Recovery was slow. In 1938, Milton Ferguson talked of a Brooklyn Public Library budget increase equal to $0.001 per capita (R35). This municipal magnanimity came at a time when, after forty years of construction delays caused by money shortages, the main library building had finally been sufficiently completed that operations could be transferred to it from the Montague Branch, where they had been housed for decades. Ferguson had been asking for extra funds to equip and staff the new headquarters building for several years, pointing out that the Montague Branch could not be stripped to equip the central building.

As the years passed, one budget after another was reported restored. At the end of the decade, only Franklin Price of Philadelphia was still indicating that disasters were yet to be faced, and he spoke more to the point of never catching up than of encountering new fiscal difficulties as a result of the depression (R159).

CHAPTER FOUR 75

*Categories Relating to the Library As An Institution*

The group of categories relating to the library as an institution received average attention from the library directors. These categories concerned library management in such areas as book selection, book supply, job classification, planning, personnel, salaries, and so on. Among them, the most attention was accorded to salaries and pensions, closely followed by book supply, with half again as much interest in personnel and in increase and reduction of services.[122]

Attention to these categories was slow and steady throughout the depression, with the exceptions of the years 1931 and 1933, when annual reports did not reflect much concern with salaries, although articles did. In 1937 and 1938, when salaries improved, annual reports also commented on the upswing. Book supply concern was strongest during the period of greatest budget cutbacks, from 1932 to 1936, since the directors worried that the increased circulation rate then current would exhaust collections through wearing out and discards without ongoing book replacement. Reductions and increases in service received about three-fifths of the interest accorded to book supply, with high concern limited to the first half of the decade, when reductions were imposed increasingly. The few mentions of increases in service in the second half of the decade merely discussed the restoration of suspended services or the inauguration of others previously untried, such as aggressively seeking ways to help business and commerce (J154).

---

[122] See Appendix IV-C, pp. 210-15.

Annual reports were the sources of ninety percent of comments on reductions and increases in the services provided, of eighty-five percent of the comments on book supply, of sixty-eight percent of the comments on personnel, but of only forty-three percent of the comments on salaries and pensions.[123] Increasing professional attention in articles was given to salaries and pensions, particularly to pensions after the announcement in January 1933 of the American Library Association-Metropolitan Life Insurance Company retirement annuity plan.[124] The discussions were not of *faits accomplis;* they were ongoing comment on viable and changing issues that took place in the journals of the profession. Many were attempts to inform or answer questions asked by other librarians rather than efforts to inform constituencies or to convince boards of directors. Concern with book supply and with services, on the other hand, were essentially matters to be drawn to the board's attention, especially since the annual report served informally as a part of budget justification. Thus, salary discussions in periodicals were more for comparison of notes than for discussion of strategy.

*Library as an Institution*

Attention was paid by library directors to the general subject of the library as an institution, but because those statements about libraries tended to be generalized and were among a wide variety of subjects and over a full range of time, it is impossible to relate them specifically to any directors or to any organizing principles. For in-

---

[123] See Appendix IV-C, Totals by Category, p. 211.
[124] See Appendix IV-C, pp. 210-211.

stance, in 1933, Clarence Sherman claimed that the depression's change and the problems that it caused would probably be with libraries for a quarter of a century, a statement he lived to see proven true (R196). Also, Harry Miller Lydenberg, in 1933, urged that librarians offer for adoption by their boards, resolutions protecting library budgets from cutting in the event that general municipal budget reductions had to be made (J123). In 1934, Sherman said that R. L. Duffus' book *Our Starving Libraries* tended to overpraise libraries and librarians in general although many of his comments were well taken and of value to the public if only the public would read them (J162). At about the same time, George Bowerman in an article suggested that elementary school libraries be eliminated on the grounds that they were inefficient, were not cost beneficial, and were quickly eliminated anyhow when school boards attempted to cut costs. Writing in *School and Society*, Bowerman proposed that strengthened public library programs geared to the needs of elementary school children be substituted for elementary school libraries (J17). It is noteworthy that no response, either of support or attack, was elicited by his proposal although there was ample opportunity for doing so.

In his presidential address to the American Library Association in 1937, Malcolm Wyer called the librarian the enduring link between the inquiring mind and books (J200). In 1939, while reviewing *Current Issues in Library Administration* by Carleton Joeckel, Carl Vitz commented that the area of library administration had not advanced very far (J178). That same year, Judson Jennings said that books related to the depression were no longer the most popular in his library (R232). These comments came from a series of statements that progressively acquired depression coloration, even though many of the subjects had no depression-orientation.

*Personnel*

Early comments on personnel were mixed; they either reflected inability to fill vacancies as they occurred or indicated a surplus of excellent candidates for every vacancy, or betrayed a smug complacency with the stability of library incomes in the face of national economic chaos (R130, R211). As time passed, salaries were reduced and staffs were cut to accommodate depression-related budget cuts. Then complaints about staff numerical inadequacy increased (R34, R174, R175, R247, R250).

The need for specialized training drew comment from a number of quarters. In 1932, Neill Unger of Portland said that all librarians needed a systematic course to qualify them to deal with the scholarly demands of many of the patrons (J175). Clarence Sherman added a year later that such a course might best be conducted by the library itself, defending the training class on grounds that its curriculum was best geared to local needs and that it afforded a lengthy evaluation period for potential recruits to the service (J167). And finally, in Los Angeles County, Helen Vogleson noted that the switch in reader interest from fiction to non-fiction demanded that many more subject specialists be on the library staff (R113).

Growing interest in state and federal aid had implications for personnel certification. In 1935, Charles Compton said that if libraries were to expect state aid, they must accept certification; both Judson Jennings and Harold Brigham indicated that certification was a guarantor of quality (J50, J27, J104).

# CHAPTER FOUR 79

Through the middle years of the decade, many directors noted the need for larger staffs to meet the growing range and volume of service demand. Increasing requests for reference service in general and for adult advisory service under which the public library employees worked; and Neill Unger at Portland spelled out the details of a needed staff-and-salary schedule (R34, J108, R190).

Personnel had begun to emerge as a specific area of interest within the general area of librarianship. It commanded steady attention throughout the decade with neither noticeable peaks nor valleys in total attention, although the foci of attention may have shifted from the beginning through the end of the decade.[125]

The difficult problems of job classification attracted considerable attention at the time, partly because relief workers were replacing some paid staff members, raising questions about whether staff members were professional or clerical (J30, R52). Furthermore, the demise of the personnel training classes that many libraries had maintained made it important for library directors to evaluate staff positions to determine whether they were professional, and hence to be filled by the graduates of library schools, or clerical, to be filled by local personnel agencies. The debate really did not achieve much distinction during the thirties, the only detailed comments on the professional and clerical distinctions being made by Clara Herbert, author of the 1939 book *Personnel Administration in Public Libraries,* and Bowerman's replacement as director at the end of the decade (J99, J100). Adam Strohm pointed out that the employees of the Detroit Public Library succeeded by working with employees of other municipal

---

[125] See Appendix IV-C, pp. 210-215.

departments in getting a workable job classification system, with salaries appropriate for the classification levels (R88).

*Salaries, Pensions, Etc.*

Perhaps no other category was as sensitive to economic conditions as that relating to the renumeration of library employees. At no time during the decade did it command primary attention of the directors of the sample. On the other hand, its continued presence showed an unwillingness of the problem of salaries to evaporate.[126]

Early in the decade, much of the concern was with salaries themselves, and attention to the category was, predictably enough, not directed to the boards of directors of libraries. Rather, the directors wrote for each other and printed their comments in the journals of the profession. As the decade progressed and salaries improved, the directors called the improvements to the attention of the boards, discussing them in annual reports.

At the same time, the American Library Association and the Metropolitan Life Insurance Company were negotiating and developing a retirement program for librarians, who previously had had indifferent coverage at best (J23, J28, J29). Annual reports and journal articles discussed the merits of the program and urged entry. As the decade passed, and the New Deal made social security coverage available to millions who had earlier had no pensions, pressure for the acceptance of the library plan increased in the journals, especially since benefits of the federal programs did not extend to librarians (J22). In

---

[126] Ibid.

1937 and 1938, many librarians described the programs in which they and the staffs of their libraries had been enabled, through municipal or state action, to participate (J172, J185, R17, R34, R74, R88, R136, R179).

Brigham had written early in the decade that a survey showed that professional leaders lacked interest in the salaries of the rank and file members of the staffs they directed (J21). Reactions by those same leaders throughout the depression to matters of salary seemed to indicate that they changed somewhat; their interest in returning salaries to the levels they had achieved before the depression was indicated often (J41, J50, J53, J146, J147, R25, R32, R33, R34, R68, R158). They did not, however, show a similar general concern for municipal action on pensions. They urged individual action, but merely reported municipal or state action. Only a few librarians seemed to have urged their boards to provide pensions for aging employees, among them Sherman and Ferguson (R29, R194).

*Recruitment, Unemployment, and Unions*

During the thirties, librarians were singularly uninterested in discussions concerning recruiting. The only comment on recruiting was that it should be limited since salaries and unemployment were more pressing problems, but that the profession should try to attract more effective people, particularly as children's librarians (J13, J14). Bowerman made the most comments on recruiting, part of his efforts being directed to increasing professionalism by discouraging people who lacked the necessary force to perform creditably, competently, and professionally from entering into the profession.

Strangely enough, the problem of unemployment among librarians did not attract much attention in this sample of directors; all the interest appeared in professional journals in 1933 and 1934, with the major concern being the extent of unemployment (J55). Two thousand unemployed librarians in the United States or fourteen unemployed librarians for every vacancy showed that unemployment among librarians was growing, and many vacant positions were left unfilled. (J10, K54). Harold Brigham even proposed that in view of the over-supply of librarians that library schools ought to raise their standards to curtail the supply of potential librarians (J25).

If unemployment was one labor-related problem during the depression, another was unionization of librarians. Unions for librarians had been subjects of controversy for a number of years before Philip O. Kenney lost his job as librarian as a result of his attempts to get the American Federation of Teachers in Montana State University in 1937 (J77). Milton Ferguson did not give Keeney the defense he gave Anna Price in 1936 when she lost her job as administrative head of the Illinois State Library (J80). Cautiously, he suggested that the American Library Association should study such cases very carefully. In his presidential speech before the ALA in 1938, Ferguson expressed happiness and relief that librarians had rejected the temptation to bring unions into libraries, thereby angering many pro-union librarians (J83). However, he welcomed the extensive objections to his comments, feeling quite sincerely that if he had a right to advise comment in opposition to unions, that as president of the national organization, he similarly had to protect the rights of all who opposed him to be heard (J88). They were heard.

CHAPTER FOUR 83

Clarence Sherman, who sided with Ferguson on unions, had probably more to say on the subject of unions than any other writer in the sample. In a 1940 article about the Third Action Committee of the American Library Association, he attacked its conclusions that libraries should have unions (J168). A few months earlier in another article, he pointed out that the strike was an ineffective tool for library employees (J169).

Library interest in unions did not specifically accompany attention generated by concern about Section VII of the National Industrial Recovery Act or the content of the Wagner Act which gave labor the right to strike. Rather, a great deal of library interest occurred even before the invalidation of NIRA in 1935 and even after the Supreme Court found the Wagner Act constitutional in 1938. And library attacks on unions had nothing whatever to say on the issues advanced and attacked in the legal decisions involved.

*Political Interference with Personnel*

There was widespread agreement among librarians that librarians were underpaid professionals and that a sense of dedication to their profession provided them with a substitute for money. Librarians responded, therefore, with shock and dismay, when they discovered that political spoilsmen were interested in their positions. Harold Brigham was one of the earliest to call attention to the problem in 1931 when he indicated that there was growing pressure to hire local people to fill any library vacancies that might arise (J24). In 1932, Daniel D. Moore's article describing libraries and library services in New Orleans, and written while he was still head of the New

Orleans Public Library, was published in the *Library Journal* with the footnote that Moore's self-perpetuating library board had been replaced by a mayor-appointed council, that Moore had resigned as director and had been replaced by a local attorney who had a four-year appointment at a salary of $7,500 per annum, which was more than six times the compensation of the best paid professional library department head who earned a mere $1,200 per annum (J129).

After a hiatus of some four years, a rash of library firings and political hirings showed that political interference had suddenly come to a head in 1936 and 1937. The gadfly who drew the attention of the profession to many of the hirings and firings was Milton J. Ferguson, librarian at Brooklyn Public Library. In a series of *Library Journal* editorials in 1936, Ferguson commented on the governor of Massachusetts, James M. Curley, giving the state Democratic women the right to select the new state librarian in 1936 from among their ranks, in the person of their president; on the firing of Anna Price, for many years the head of the Illinois State Library, after Price had succeeded in getting the political plum of state aid money to distribute; on the firing in Cicero, Illinois of a competent librarian and his replacement with a political hack; and on the firing of the New Brunswick, New Jersey librarian and on his replacement by the Board president, a bankrupt tailor who was also working on a history project under the auspices of the WPA (J85, J84, J76).

At about the same time, a judge in New Orleans ruled against a local effort to restrict the candidacy for the position of head of the New Orleans Public Library to local people (J86). Thus, renewal of the attempt to reappoint a political hanger-on in New Orleans (after the four-year tenure of the lawyer) was eventually defeated, for the courts required that the local board hire a competent librarian. Governor Curley, who thought state librarianship could be filled by a high school graduate whose only experience was in homemaking, lost in the 1936 election when he ran for the Senate of the United States (J81).

Evidence of new spoilsmanship also appeared in 1937 when the governor of Iowa replaced the late state librarian with a local Democrat whose chief distinction was unsuccessful candidacy for many state offices (J93) Ferguson ridiculed the practice of certain boards of appointing from among their own membership by calling it "an old New England custom," a label that elicited the ire of Milton Lord, the librarian of the Boston Public Library, who cited his predecessor, Justin Winsor, as the epitome of excellence in librarianship and a board member before becoming a librarian (J87, J116). Thereafter, Ferguson produced no more editorials on the subject.

*Categories Accorded Less Attention*

Book binding and book mending commanded article comment from Anne Mulheron, who had left the Portland Library Association to become head of the Oregon WPA Library Project, and from L.L. Dickerson of the Indianapolis Public Library (J66, J130). The noisiest imbroglio of the era that was carried out in library publications concerned the book binding activities of WPA workers. Pelham Barr of the Library Binding Institute denounced the quality of "binding work" performed by WPA employed library clerks. He contended that the WPA took business from commercial binderies and employment from their staffs. Many librarians, however, countered that the work done by the WPA would not have gone to commercial binderies anyway: either the libraries had no funds for sending books to binderies, or the need was simply to mend and clean, neither a bindery task. Dickerson also commented that when adequate supervision was available, WPA people did an adequate job, thus answering Barr's charges about quality (J66).

In a fairly early article on library cooperation, Malcolm Wyer discussed the Denver Bibliographic Center, where the libraries in the sparsely settled mountain states cooperated to build a bibliographic center and to acquire materials that none of them could have afforded alone (J203).

An unpleasant situation developed during the American Library Association Annual Conference in 1936, which was held in Richmond, Virginia. Negro librarians were required to sit in special sections of the auditoria and to miss meal portions of dinner meetings. Many librarians from all kinds of libraries, including Beatrice Winser and Carl Roden from this sample, wrote protesting the treatment of the Negro librarians in Richmond (J153, J194, K195). The only defender of the practice as it was evidenced at the ALA meeting was Jesse Cunningham of the Memphis Cossit Library (J63). He stated, first, that segregation of Negroes was a southern problem and that southerners should be allowed to solve it; second, that northern librarians who objected to southern practices were attempting to impose their practices on southern people in a most ungracious manner; and third, that northern Negroes were far fewer in number and hence, less a problem. So far as this author has been able to find out, only Miss Winser answered Cunningham. She said that she was not attempting to tell southern people how to treat the Negro minority; she merely felt that the American Library Association should not subject its members to the treatment that would be accorded them in certain cities of the south (J195). The last word in the controversy went to Roden, who reported that the ALA should not henceforth meet in any city where all members were not treated equally, a statement that seemed to close the issue (J153).

Tommie Dora Barker, by now Dean of the Emory Library School, responded to a 1938 *Library Journal* editorial, which had drawn attention to male domination of upper level administrative positions. Barker decried the fact that the editorial statement was all too true (J5). She showed that women did not get a fair number of positions on the ALA nominating committees, that very few women were nominated for elective office, and that they did not get adequate representation or a proportionate number of positions in the upper echelons among the appointive positions.

Bernard Berelson's 1952 study of content analysis admits the occasional necessity of a heading called *Other* or *Miscellaneous* for stray bits of information that could not be squeezed into any of the existing categories. Examples of these were mentioned in the articles and annual reports in the thirties. For example: Milton Ferguson once indicated that the library staff contributed one percent of six months' salary for relief of the unemployed; Carl Roden reported that transaction charging had been installed in the Chicago Public Library branches; Clarence Sherman described the library publicity efforts and problems; Ferguson bemoaned the inability to establish centralized registration so as to eliminate the book stealers who stole from the library's branches; Brigham and Sherman engaged in an altercation about the efficacy of the training class; and Bowerman reported that a contract had been let for a new library building in the District of Columbia (R27, R28, R49, R193, J18, J32, J167). This miscellany reflects only brief interest in one-time, once-treated subjects, such interest being limited to only a single director, or at the most two, who contributed briefly on the subject to the universe.

*Categories Relating to the Library in its Socio-Political Setting*

Directors divided their attention between the twin facets of this group of categories: on the one hand where those categories such as federal aid and state aid to libraries and on the other hand categories on the library as a branch of government that pertained in one way or another to the newly important role of the library as a political institution. In general, they were the occasions of far more questions and, in some cases, controversy, than were the far more familiar discussions of the library's role and problems in service its public.

With many of these categories, long professional service had acquainted the directors with the routine characteristics of the category, except that the special problems created by the depression were new. It is to the novel problems, the by-products of the depression, that this study addresses itself.

*Government-Related Categories*

The most vitriolic exchanges in the professional print were occasioned by federal aid to education and to libraries. Librarians who are part of the sample commented on the subject from 1933 until 1939, but no great interest was generated until the New Deal programs started to provide federal aid to various agencies, programs, and activities.[127] Once the national government was recognized as a possible source of funds for many previously unsupported library programs, the profession began choosing sides on the issue of whether federal aid was in truth beneficial or detrimental to libraries.

The earliest, the most prophetic comment was by Milton J. Ferguson, who said in 1933 that federal aid was not and would not be a reality for some time (J82). While he professed delight in the recommendations of the Reeves Committee[128] that favored federal aid to libraries in 1938, he neither anticipated nor planned on the implementation of the potential bonanza of the federal aid bill to libraries, neither did he support actively the Harrison-Thomas-Fletcher bill which was the congressional vehicle for the recommendations of the Reeves Committee (J74).

Other writers, however, were not so reticent. Charles Compton, president of the American Library Association in 1934 when the first recommendations regarding federal aid were approved by the professional association, wrote frequently in favor of it (J36, J46, J50). Judson Jennings of Seattle, long proponent of state aid, thought it would be too little, too late (J104). Carl Vitz, by then of Minneapolis, had a personal campaign in favor of federal aid going on throughout the latter part of the decade. He supported proponents of federal aid, attacked its opponents, and defended Carleton Joeckel's findings in *Library Service* that federal aid to libraries was virtually a necessity (J179, J183, J184). Ralph Munn supported federal aid on the

---

[127] See Appendix IV-C, pp. 210-15.
[128] See Chapter II, pp. 39-41.

theoretical ground that it would tend to equalize library service for all Americans while Louis E. Bailey of Queens said that federal aid was necessary because only the federal government had the taxing power required for substantial library support (J2, J137). Many other librarians in the library journals argued about the merits and demerits of federal aid even more vehemently, but it did not become a reality in the thirties. The earliest federal aid to libraries was in the *Library Services Act* in 1956, and the funding it gave was minimal and limited to rural areas, defined as communities with fewer than 10,000 people.

The problem of a federal library agency was less violently argued, but it generated interest among librarians and resulted in many taking sides on the issue. Among the librarians of this sample, Compton of St. Louis defended the idea of a federal agency almost as much as he defended federal aid (J34). He attempted to demonstrate that a federal library agency would be at least as beneficial to libraries as the Office of Education was to education in America. When the American Library Association endorsed the idea of a federal library agency, Beatrice Winser accused it of abjuring its professional responsibilities to the federal library agency, which she considered a "fascistic idea" and a totally unnecessary one, leading to a waste of money (J192). The functions of the proposed federal library agency, she claimed, are inherent functions and responsibilities of local librarians in the proper exercise of their professional duties.

During the nineteen thirties, even though the importance of the government in the lives of libraries was manifest, public libraries seemed unaware that they existed also as branches of government. Only the Washington D.C. Library and the Seattle Public Library made any

CHAPTER FOUR 91

attempt to demonstrate their service to other municipal agencies, by showing, year by year, which portion of their business was devoted to other branches of the government that served the citizens of the municipality (R223-233, R244-253).

Among the many statements on the codes of the National Recovery Administration, the librarians in the sample produced three. The first comment expressed the fear that the NRA binding code would raise the cost of binding, and lower the number of books that could be sent to the bindery; the second commented on the attempts of retail booksellers to eliminate discounts to libraries, an effort that failed; and the third concerned an effort by some librarians to develop for the profession a code of ethics much like those being developed by NRA, especially in the specific areas of salary and fringe benefits (J109, R52, R196). John Boynton Kaiser, the librarian at Oakland Public Library, wrote one article on this category. The lack of any follow-up articles seemed to indicate that the ruling of the Supreme Court invalidating most of the National Recovery Act may have reduced considerably the drive for an NRA-type of code for librarians.

Of the host of federal programs, apart from the work relief programs that have already been mentioned, only the Public Works Administration had been sought in the construction of library branches in the Washington, D.C. Public Library, as well as in the enlargement of the main building (R247, R252). Sherman also mentioned that the city council in Providence had rejected an effort by the library to seek PWA help in securing a new building (R197, R199). Little other comment on library efforts to work with the PWA surfaced among the writings of these directors.

Judson Jennings spoke out the most on the need for state aid, especially in his annual reports of 1935, 1937, and 1940, and in three articles on the subject (J103, J104, J105, R228, R230, R233). None of the acrimony and emotionalism that characterized discussions on federal aid appeared with state aid. Libraries simply recognized the greater ability of the states to tax and looked to them for the revenue their cities could no longer provide. Ralph Munn of Pittsburgh wrote that state aid and the state library agencies were vital in equalizing access to library service (J137). Numerous librarians also reported expenditures of state aid. Roden of Chicago, Strohm of Detroit, and Hamilton of Dayton reported the receipts, expenditures, and fluctuations in the amounts of state aid their individual libraries received (R55, R74, R88). But Jennings, the most fervent advocate of state aid, did not manage to get it for his library, for legislative appropriations for state aid in both 1937 and 1940 were vetoed (R230, R233). Strohm reported that the associate librarian of Detroit, Ralph Ulveling, helped secure the first state aid appropriations in Michigan and that more money was hoped for in future appropriations (R88). As a rule, librarians who favored state aid had state legislators as their antagonists, not other librarians.

*Categories Related to Public Service*

The librarians of the sample paid attention to the library's place in a society that suddenly was rapidly and radically changed. They discussed the libraries' efforts to help people learn to cope with a society for which their experience did not prepare them.[129] This category occupied the attention of library directors throughout the decade, but principally through the first two-thirds of it, with the last year being devoted to the social problem, not of the depression, but rather of war.

In 1932, 1933, and 1934, statements on the importance of libraries were stressed, for libraries were essential for those who wished to learn new skills, and for those who needed some sort of reading material to raise their spirits and morale (R29, R84, R173, J10, J20, J58, J158). As time passed, concern shifted from the new book needs of burgeoning library patronage to the inability of libraries to cope with such expanding needs, an inability so serious as to lose whatever new readers had been gained (R23, J167).

Comments in the areas of public relations, when mentioned in the annual reports, were perfunctory listings of such matters as how may newspaper articles were published, how many booklists were produced for distribution, how many book talks were given, etc.—all of which could have appeared irrespective of the depression. The articles produced for journal publication provided more suggestions. The best article was written by Carl Vitz, who regarded public relations as a tool in the budget campaign and the budget campaign as a year-long effort (J180). He suggested that all people who could have a voice in the budget decision be given all the information that they might use in decision making and further, that the librarian go to the budget hearings armed with all manner of comparison: how much the library spent in a year compared with one department or other, or a com-

---

[129] See Appendix IV-C, pp. 210-15.

parison of per capita per annum library expenditures with those of some other municipal department or with some frequently made expenditures of the people, such as cigarettes. Vitz did not, however, recommend cultivating party leaders for advancing library purposes. As a special public relations effort, the Chicago Public Library went on the radio in 1936 with a number of broadcasts featuring its special services (J151). From Minneapolis, Gratia Countryman pointed out that the best possible public relations in the time of the crisis was a widespread demonstration of the library's ability to aid people in coping with the problems that the depression had brought them (J161).

Libraries paid attention to some special groups, principally children and youth. They pointed out that service to children from public libraries had probably raised the quality of service to children (J12, J160). It was only in the last half of the decade, after the worst budget cuts had been made, that there were discussions of reducing service to children, but no actual widespread policy of reductions of service specifically to children seem to have taken place; disastrous budget reductions and book supply curtailments may have hit service to children more.

Russel Schunk of Toledo suggested that libraries pay more attention to meeting the special needs of the businessmen whose taxes paid much of the bill for library service, while Paul Paine described the WPA-sponsored shut-in service that had been developed as a special service at the Syracuse Public Library (J144, J154).

Accorded great attention during the depression was the importance of reading. A number of librarians insisted upon the highest reading quality of materials and books and spoke out in this category, among them Clarence

Sherman (R193, R194, J159). He said that the library's first duty was to help in building morale, to train people for new vocations, and to help inform and teach people about the crisis through which they were passing (R194). Sherman coupled these injunctions with another: that in an age where the population wanted immediate gratifications of all whims, the library's responsibility was to strive to maintain quality (R193). Four years later, in 1935, he had grown pessimistic about the library's role in educating the public through reading quality (J159). Except "for stimulation and excitement," reading was not valued by the masses, only by scholars. He regretted that librarians held the reader of mystery stories equal in value with the scholar, for the latest bestseller counted exactly as much for circulation purposes as did the most illuminating tome of scholarship.

In contrast, Adam Strohm of Detroit enthusiastically commented that more borrowers were constantly improving, and that materials of high quality were being used by borrowers (R82, R83). Strohm felt that the intrinsic value of good books was important everywhere, and that the public libraries were becoming a basic source—where questions may be resolved and answers found by the general public. In 1935, he declared that good fiction was of greater value than pedestrian nonfiction with the importance of content being the major consideration, a unique comment among the writings of librarians during the period. In 1940, he reaffirmed that good reading, including good fiction, was therapeutic for readers (J910).

Two middle-of-the-roaders on this category were Malcolm Wyer and Milton J. Ferguson. Wyer affirmed that important books, whether classics or the best productions of the contemporary press, needed to be read;

Ferguson saw libraries in an age of social and political crisis as an aid to the people's survival (J79, J200). Of all the library directors, Strohm had to face the severest budget cuts, but he remained the most optimistic.

When the list of categories was being developed, it was discovered that there was sufficient interest in unserved people in the writings of librarians outside the sample to justify inclusion of that category. The sample itself showed that the category was needed, but for another population: those living within service areas of metropolitan libraries, but so far from any branch that service was not really within reach. Foremost among the librarians interested in the subject were Price of Philadelphia, Bowerman of the District of Columbia, and Mun of Pittsburgh Carnegie Library (J140, R155, R157, R158, R181, R248). The extension of service beyond the corporate limits of the municipality was discussed by a number of librarians, most of whom agreed that such service should not be a gift, but must be paid for (R174, R243). There was general agreement that librarians had no right to give away what their constituents had purchased, and making potential constituents pay for such services as the library could offer was the only way to encourage new patrons to value them properly. Paul Paine of Syracuse pointed out, however, that few supervisors in rural areas would probably be willing to pay for such rural library service when very few residents were likely to take advantage of it (R243).

Librarians, as custodians of public property, were often incensed by the public's failure to treat that property properly. Many of them wrote throughout the decade of their agitation over the failure of borrowers to respect what they had borrowed, through vandalism, willful destruction, and theft (R31, R34, R37, R193, R197, R198). Only Sherman reported a substantial drop in the amount of book theft; most librarians reported the rising of book theft (R2010. After commenting annually during the first third of the decade that too many books were being stolen and too many were being borrowed by people who did not return them, he said in 1938 that a drop had taken place in book theft. Ralph Munn attributed the problem to the severe breakdown in morale caused by World War I and the depression, a breakdown that in part accounted for the increase in theft (J141).

All the librarians insisted that the vandalism, destruction, and theft should stop, but no one could propose any workable final solution to the problem. Exit control was considered the most effective method of reducing book theft, but even that was of limited effectiveness to someone determined to circumvent it (J141, R34).

A controversy over fine cancellation week or conscience week split the profession briefly in late 1932 and early 1933. Essentially, libraries attempted to reinstate suspended borrowers after they had accumulated fines and had lost their borrowing privileges, or had kept books long overdue and could not return them because they were not able to pay the fines. During conscience week, delinquent borrowers could be reinstated simply by returning the overdue books, or by requesting that their suspensions be lifted. Clarence Sherman and Chalmers Hadley violently opposed allowing the return of books without fines or the reinstitution of borrowing privileges in cases where they had been suspended, both on the grounds that lawabiding library patrons did not have problems with overdue books and accumulated fines, and therefore would be the losers; only those who disregarded library borrowing regulations would benefit (J95, R195). Other people who approved the idea generally did so on simple humanitarian grounds: books were greatly needed, especially in a time of severe economic and spiritual distress. Certain people could not borrow books because of a rule; the simplest solution was to suspend the rule. The quarrel was brief, enduring only a few months late in 1932 and early in 1933. It did not achieve common settlement: some librarians attempted fine suspension weeks and returned some borrowers to the active list; others did not. Some librarians regretted seeing borrowing privileges restored to some of their worst trouble-makers but the issue faded away after a few months, not to occur again in the study's sample. In all probability, people went on accumulating library fines, and either libraries had fine cancellation weeks in silence or the idea was abandoned.

*Categories Related to Economic Conditions*

Librarians as a rule eschewed general comments on economic matter relating to the depression, and only two from the sample made special references to the economy, albeit peripherally. Ann Muheron, in 1936, observed that the depression was apparently over because salaries were going up and more staff could be hired (R188). Arthur Bostwick, in 1935, indicated that the overall recovery from the depression was slow and that library recovery was even slower (J214). Other comments concerned the library's operations in adult education, in teaching people what depression means; in acquisitions, because of the fluctuations in the dollar's value vis-à-vis that of foreign currencies; in materials, in their being harder to buy than a year previous (J82, R133, R246).

No substantial article or series of articles on the depression and libraries appear written by librarians, nor did articles on the depression as it affected the layman appear in library literature could deal with it (J24, J132, J171, R72, R78, R84, R173, R189). They wrote extensively about fees and economies as practical measures to combat the depression, with two-thirds of the comments appearing in annual reports.[130] Most comments on fees and economies was limited to a recital of those purchases or activities that had been either eliminated or curtailed so as to reduce the outflow of money. Fees were few; librarians preferred to rent new fiction rather than to lend it. The renting of books, however, was illegal in Ohio; so as to circumvent this ruling, the free loan period for new fiction was limited to one day, whereafter, an overdue book fee was charged (R72).

Changes usually were made through a series of budget reductions: first, on supplies and maintenance; second, on book funds; and third, on salaries. Clarence Sherman in Providence attempted to make only changes that could be accepted on a permanent basis (J165). A significant change brought on for reasons of economy was transaction charging in which book charge slips are filed by transaction rather than by title, author, or call number and which extensively involves the patron in creating the slip, hence 1) reducing filing time considerably and 2) cutting down on catalog department typing. The Detroit Public Library also started charging rental for non-fiction (patterned after rentals for fiction) so as to provide nonfiction that could not otherwise be purchased (J171). Many small, nuisance variety changes were instituted in

---

[130] See Appendix IV-C, pp. 210-15.

the name of economy, such as charges for postcards indicating availability of reserved books and registration fees (R189). Early in the depression, cuts in building maintenance budgets and capital outlay were listed, but once those cuts became permanent, further mentions of them were infrequent.

Most discussions by librarians of general finance centered around the discussions of budget. That is to say, they discussed per capita expenditures in comparison with the expenditures of other libraries, or they talked about the need to increase the budget if the library were to maintain its position and not be worn out by its service load, or they discussed the lack of a book fund, the inadequacy of state aid, or the way they could get some capital outlay funds from their endowments (J25, J166, R40, R54, R91, R194, R199). Discussions of finances were in general directed more toward library boards than toward other libraries. Hence they appeared usually in annual reports.[131] The content of the material on this category was not especially illuminating except to show that librarians in general knew little in the area of municipal finance.

In contrast to their vague statements on municipal finances, librarians seemed capable, in general, of making accurate assessments concerning taxes and taxation. Linda Eastman, in Cleveland's 1931 annual report, correctly foresaw problems with the Ohio municipal taxes for librarians and predicted that those problems would lead to cuts in the budget (R62). Carl Roden, at about the same time, stated that Illinois had a problem similar to Ohio's (J152). A lawsuit had delayed the collection of real

---

[131] See Appendix IV-C, pp. 210-15.

estate taxes in Illinois for eighteen months, so much so that the library had had to borrow on anticipated tax revenue for operating expenses, and many problems ensued. The problems with municipal taxes were major for other Ohio librarians during the decade. In 1932, Will Collins of Akron commented on the substantial delinquency in the collection of the intangibles tax,[132] which had been substituted for the property tax that had previously supported Ohio's libraries (R1). In 1933, Eastman pointed out that Ohio tax problems had been settled but that the consequent problems would remain for some time (J70, R64).

Some librarians had gone through a period of no income; many had spent their capital outlay funds for operations. Their inadequate book budgets precluded the acquisition of important materials that needed to be added to their collections. These problems would remain with libraries for years, they could not be met with instant solutions and unlimited funds. Commenting on the problems of taxation two years later, in 1935, Paul North Rice of Dayton expressed a low opinion of the intelligence of politicians who allowed the tax difficulties to develop (R75).

Toward the middle of the decade, considerations ranged from the specific problem of property tax delinquency to the inadequacy of the income derived from it, to other possible sources of revenue, particularly that of state aid. Problems of taxation as a rule were accompanied by speculations about new sources of revenue, and

---

[132] Ohio libraries are supported by a tax on intangible property such as stocks and bonds.

librarians inevitably turned to the state legislatures for help. In many cases, they also turned to Washington.

*Comments on Time-Span, Source, and Director Attitude Toward Material*

In the discussion of categories in this section of the fourth chapter, comment was made from time to time about the chronological range of the categories; where there was no such comment, it is to be understood that the range was decade-long. Where the information seemed relevant, interesting, or useful, director preference for either annual reports or articles was also noted.

A number of broad generalizations about the foci of attention may be illuminating. First, the directors said nearly three times as much in annual reports as they did in periodical articles. The ratio was not consistent across category types, however; in discussions of the library's status vis-à-vis its public and government, the ratio was about five to one favoring annual reports. In discussions of the economic situation, nearly the same ratio held; each mention in an article was countered by almost four in annual reports. Only in discussions of the library as an institution where the ratio was about three to two, did a near-balance between annual reports and periodicals obtain.

Over fifty percent of all comments in periodical articles appeared in the *American Library Association Bulletin*. The *Library Journal* was second with nearly forty percent. With such a preponderance for the two leading periodicals, little remained for the others. It was divided thus: *Journal of Adult Education* and *Library Quarterly* had about four percent each, and *Libraries, School and Society, Wilson Library*

*Bulletin,* and *Special Libraries* divided the remaining four percent.

The generalizations were not equally true, however, for each of the three large classes of categories. In the first, pertaining to the library as an institution, the overall ratio held firm. But in discussions of the economy, the *American Library Association Bulletin* was by far the periodical of choice; comments in it out-numbered those in the *Library Journal* by a ratio of 2.73 to 1.

Discussions of the library as part of a society and of a government, however, produced a vastly different pattern of preference. *The American Library Association Bulletin* and the *Library Journal* continued to provide about ninety percent of the information, but in this one class of categories, the *Library Journal* was preferred to the *American Library Association Bulletin* by a ratio of about six to five.

The appealing prospect of protracted games with numbers relating to preference must be curtailed, for the basic ratios, once established, are the only ones that matter. The ratios are two: annual reports were favored for 75 percent of the comments. Of the journals, the *American Library Association Bulletin* was preferred in 50 percent of the cases, especially for matters such as the library as an institution and economic conditions. For discussion of the library's relations with its public, the *Library Journal* was preferred 54 percent of the time.

Reasons for these preferences do not appear within the universe. External data, however, might support certain tentative conclusions. On the unnumbered page opposite its Table of Contents, each issue of the *American Library Association Bulletin* stated that it "[...] carries news of the Association, its officers, boards, committees, sections, and staff; addresses of conference speakers; articles of official representatives of the Association; and brief professional communications to or from members. Its scope does not include articles on library matters unrelated to the Association." The membership to which the *Bulletin* was sent numbered about 15,600. The *Library Journal*, whose circulation was about one third as large, was not hindered by the confines of this stated editorial policy. Mr. John Berry, editor of the *Journal*, affirmed that its purpose has remained the same since stated by Melville Dewey in the *Journal*'s first issue in September 1876, namely, the promotion of any effort that would tend to improve the practice of librarianship. Mr. Berry stated, "The magazine has always existed with absolute editorial freedom. There has been no censorship by management."[133]

Sophisticated analyses exceeding the scope of this study might reveal relationships between the output of the librarians who constitute the sample of the economic conditions that elicited the comments. Generally, however, one can offer little comparison between periodical article comment and economic conditions. Comments on depression-related matters in annual reports peaked in 1934 and 1937, two of the worst years for the economy. As tax collections dropped, librarian-authors seem to have stopped writing articles, for 1934 and 1937 were low output years. Other generalizations are fraught with peril, especially the shift to a war economy at the end of the decade makes any specific statements questionable. And problems with determining just when the impact of the depression was first felt in the libraries have been discussed: book circulation increased before budgets and

---

[133] John Berry, telephone interview with researcher on 9 April 1975.

expenditures decreased, and the effect on director output would be a reflection of the strength of the municipality's economy, the library's endowment, and the librarian's tendency to discuss his problems in print.

Content analysis revealed two rather interesting choices of periodicals. The first of these pertained to segregation of Negro librarians at the Richmond conference of the American Library Association in 1936. A rash of angry letters were occasioned by the requirement that Negroes sit in designated areas of auditoria and attend only the meeting portion of dinner programs—the letters from the librarians in this sample appeared only in the *Library Journal,* in the issues of 1 January, July, and August 1936, the *Bulletin* of the Association whose conference seemed to have published nothing, not even the signed Committee Report, which appeared in the *Library Journal,* announcing that the Association would thereafter avoid cities where all of its members would not be treated equally.

Among the eighteen comments on political interference with library personnel, especially in their selection, sixteen, or 88 percent appeared in the *Library Journal.* The American Library Association printed the other two in its *Bulletin.* The majority of the comments on the problem appeared in editorials written by Milton J. Ferguson; Harold Brigham, Arthur Bostwick, Paul North Rice, and Ralph Munn joined Ferguson in fighting the political spoilsmen. As the decade progressed, comment on political interference decreased, and Ferguson said that such interference was waning. Significantly perhaps, neither segregation of Negro librarians nor political interference with personnel was mentioned in an annual report.

*Major Contributors to the Universe*

Sketches of thirteen library directors whose contributions to the universe were the largest are offered not as assessments of careers, nor of the materials they produced during their careers, nor even of materials they produced during the depression. Rather, because this study has been concerned with depression-related contributions to annual reports and periodical articles, these comments concern their words. No comment is made as to the quality of any writer's thought, nor to the amount of reaction any statement may have evoked. Of the thirteen librarians whose ideas are sketched, seven had, by 1940, been president of the American Library Association.

The cities these library directors served are well-representative in population, expenditures, and expenditures per capita. The librarians were not exclusively from the biggest cities nor from the best-supported libraries, nor from the libraries with the largest income per capita. Indeed, Milton J. Ferguson, one of the most prolific writers, worked in a library with poor support, the Brooklyn Public Library. The librarians with the best per capita support, Linda Eastman and Charles Rush, produced little material on the depression although they wrote a good deal on other subjects during the decade. No annual reports were available from the median library in expenditures, Kansas City, and its director, Louis Nourse, wrote only one article. The median library in support per capita, Pittsburgh Allegheny, for a number of years had no annual report contributions of any substance written by its directors, nor were these articles written by either of its directors, David Cadugan or George Seibel. In his history of Carnegie Libraries, George Bobinski says of the Allegheny Library in the United States, that local pride kept the library from inclusion in the Pittsburgh system even after the annexation of the municipality, Allegheny, by Pittsburgh in 1909.[134] He added that the Allegheny Library was served by a succession of political appointees. However, no comment on either Cadugan or Seibel as political appointees was made by librarians who decried such appointments in the articles mentioned earlier.

The sketches that follow are in order by the size of the directors' contributions to the universe studied in this dissertation.

*Harry Miller Lydenberg*

The most prolific author in this sample was Harry Miller Lydenberg, librarian of the New York Public Library from 1934 until the end of the decade. His contributions to the annual reports often exceeded eighty pages (more than the directors of twenty out of the total thirty five libraries that had published annual reports produced in the decade), and the whole of the New York Public Library annual report was itself a book of several hundred pages every year. Lydenberg's articles were substantial contributions to the universe, and with so voluminous an output, his interests could be amply documented. He commented often in his annual reports on adult education, but did so only once in an article.[135] He believed that the student, not the librarian, was the teacher in an adult

---

[134] George S. Bobinski, *Carnegie Libraries: Their History and Impact on American Public Library Development* (Chicago: American Library Association, 1969), pp. 27, ix.
[135] See Appendix IV-A, p. 197.

education situation and that it was not within the proper province of the librarian to be the teacher (J125).

In 1936, along with many other librarians, he worried that readers who were being lost because desired books were unavailable would be lost permanently (R135). A year later, in 1937, he expressed a common professional concern among librarians when he complained about the use of cigarette contest competitors of reference tools to the exclusion of other users (R136). Puzzle contestants in some libraries were wearing out valuable reference tools faster than they could be replaced. His assessment of reader interest during the thirties revealed that as the decade progressed, interest shifted from the causes of the economic depression to such objects as EPIC, the Canadian Social Credit Party, Townsendism, then to Nazism, and finally, to more trivial matters such as escape reading (R133-R139).

Lydenberg wrote at great length of the contributions of federal projects to the services of the library, indicating year by year the importance of the efforts of the WPA, CWA, FERA, and NYA. On only two occasions did he complain about federal projects, and then his complaints were not on the workers assigned to the New York Library but rather on the deleterious impact on the reference room of the WPA workers sent there on bibliographic projects sponsored by other agencies (R135, R137). WPA workers who were not supervised by Lydenberg's staff were slow and did not persevere in their work; chatted too much, disturbing other workers in the library; and overcrowded the area, to the exclusion of other users of the library.

In his comments on budgets, he was no different from all the other librarians in the sample who said that their budgets were inadequate. One additional comment seemed atypical: he stated that if far too many budget commissions regard the library as a luxury, then their lack of regard for library services was the library's fault, for then librarians had failed in demonstrating the necessity of library service (J127). At one point he answered a critic of library service who wanted to make it more exclusive in the high quality of its service by claiming that the library should be open to all, not only the most serious scholars (J122). Libraries should serve all readers, he affirmed, and should particularly cultivate the young, who are then enticed to become lifetime readers. This comment was in answer to critics who claimed that library funds should not be budgeted for service to children.

*Clarence Sherman*

Clarence Sherman's overriding concern was for the quality of library service especially at the Providence, Rhode Island Public Library. He believed in having the best material available for all readers, irrespective of age, and mass service as reflected in circulation statistics was not important to him (J164). He felt that libraries, on the other hand, had been subjected to undue criticism because of their age and conservatism, while, on the other hand, they had been lavishly and undeservedly praised for certain of their more popular efforts (J156, J159, R196, R197, R200). As conservators of the intellectual tradition, their essential function, libraries should be praised, not condemned. As for making all material available to all people, a policy often widely praised, libraries that did so often attempted more than they might justifiably sustain. In Sherman's opinion, evidences of liberal policy were open stacks and patron registration that did not require a co-signer. He opposed conscience days and fine cancellation on the grounds that they were unjust to library users who conscientiously returned books when due or paid their fines (R195). That he was not a fiscal conservative, however, is evidenced by the fact that the Providence Library had one of the highest per capita rates of expenditure in its size class and that he aided efforts that led finally to pension plans for Providence Library employees (J163, R193). In his opinion, the depression was responsible for low salaries (not a surplus of librarians), and Harold Brigham was wrong in trying to raise salaries by abolishing the training class (which Brigham thought was blurring the distinction between professional and subprofessional workers), for the training class was a worthwhile institution (J167).

Although admitting that salaries were low, Sherman opposed unions of library employees on the grounds that strikes would not serve to provide the advantages that unions claimed, nor could they raise salaries in the case of library and public employees (J168, J169).

His most eloquent words were about good books and their value to people. In the worst days of the depression, in the annual report of 1934, he said that reading has endured and that it will always endure; that people will always want good books, and that librarians will always be needed to find those books for those readers (R197). His optimism persisted through the polio epidemic of 1935, the hurricane of 1938, and throughout the depression decade (R198, R201).

Sherman was one of the most forceful writers on the reaction of the library with its environment. He decried waste in any form, especially the waste of human beings and human minds through the inattention of libraries and schools in exercising their proper function in the education of youth as readers (J156, J161). This neglect must stop, he said, and young people must be made readers. In 1935, he saw that service to teenagers was not another form of children's librarianship or adult advisory service, for the needs of young adults were specialized and demanded specialized treatment (J161). Finally, as the decade advanced, Sherman grew increasingly dependent upon municipal financing (R195, R198, R201). At the beginning of the depression, he felt protected by income from the endowment of the association that supported the Providence Library; by the end of the depression, he insisted on greater municipal support for the library, although he remained opposed to federal aid and silent on state aid.

*Milton J. Ferguson*

Brooklyn Public Library's Milton J. Ferguson was, like Sherman, a prolific writer with broad interests. He led the fight against the use of library positions by political spoilsmen, who suggested that P.O. Keeney was dismissed at Montana State University for instigating efforts to organize librarians as a part of the American Federation of Teachers and then reinstated. His mild comments on unions—far milder, in fact, than Sherman's—drew a storm of protest from his professional associates, perhaps because he uttered them in an American Library Association presidential address.

His general attitude on involvement with state and federal authorities was, at best, distant. He never either attacked or endorsed state aid, but attacked the conclusions of those who seemed to regard federal aid as a cornucopia (J82). He said that if it ever came, it would not be substantial. No objections on theoretical grounds were made to using WPA workers, but in one annual report after another be commented on the poor workmanship of the men sent in for maintenance jobs, and on the slow completion of the major construction projects (R29, R31, R32, R35, R36). For the women employed on WPA clerical projects, he had a higher regard, indicating that many of them were hired to fill staff vacancies when they arose (R36). A final objection to WPA workers in general was that they could earn as much hourly, with neither college training nor experience, as Brooklyn Public Library could pay to its trained and experienced professional assistants (R32).

His complaints about budget were many, and apparently well-founded. He argued that Brooklyn Borough Public Library, Queens Borough Public Library, and the Circulation Department of the New York Public Library all justified their budgets to the same municipal commission, thus should be able to expect equal treatment on a per capita basis (R28, R32, R35). But Brooklyn received thirty-eight cents, New York, fifty cents, and Queens, seventy cents (R28). Ferguson, did not, finally, spend time in the professional print discussing matters that he considered less than important; all of his comments stated firmly their author's high regard for their claims on professional concern.

*George F. Bowerman*

Bowerman had two major interests: first, getting a new building for the District of Columbia Library to replace or supplement the over-crowded existing central library building and second, defending public library service to children. His annual reports and articles detailed the efforts to add to the quarters of the public library he directed, and his last reports jubilantly discussed the dates of readiness for occupancy and the dates for completion of his new building (R251, R252, R253). His defense of public library service to elementary school children and his attacks on libraries in elementary schools make sense even today (J12). He argued that cutting public library service to children simply reduced their preparation for life, and that putting libraries into elementary school buildings merely provided a budget that was the first target for administrators to cut. Such elementary school libraries were more costly than public library service to elementary school children. His concern about children's service extended to the librarians who provided that service, for he desired more active, less passive librarians than those whom he saw most frequently recruited as children's librarians (J13, J14).

Bowerman's belief in good books and dislike for "weakling fiction" colored his articles (J12, J16). His comments on federal programs were mostly descriptive; at no point did he attack or criticize workers for needing undue supervision or for being lackadaisical in their work attitudes and performance (R248, R249, R250, R251). There was apparently a good relationship between him and the Congress. On numerous occasions, when the Executive Budget contained a cut for the library, Congress restored the budget to at least the previous year's level (R249, R250, R251).

## Ralph Munn

Munn was an early and strong supporter of both federal and state aid channeled through state library agencies (J136). As the administrator of the Pittsburgh Carnegie Library, he perceived the need for strong state library agencies to handle federal and state grants, for he said frankly, too often state libraries were unable to handle the administration of money (J137). His other strong interests were in quality, an interest he shared with most of his colleagues, in the protection from vandalism of the materials for which he was responsible, and in extending service to the unserved, but on a basis that required of the unserved that they pay their fair share (J140, R141).

Many other library directors in this sample regretted the lack of respect for public property demonstrated by those youngsters who cut up library materials for school notebooks, who kept materials overdue or never returned them, who stole library materials, and who treated them as if they were trash. Munn traced the problems of vandalism to the breakdown in morale caused by the previous war and to the depression, and more importantly, suggested some of the means for combating vandalism. Like many other librarians, he was concerned with the large number of people who were not able to use public libraries, but he rejected totally and flatly extending service to these people free while others were paying for it through taxes (J140). He suggested that those living outside legal areas be granted service but at the price of either a borrower's fee or a contract between the governing bodies concerned; thus the service itself would be valued. Furthermore, he wanted service extended to people in

Pittsburgh where branches were inadequately distributed (R174).

In discussing budget reductions, he recommended that all lien items be cut first and that the easiest cuts be made after that (J139). His definition of an easy cut was that it was a service that was easy to restore later. In his discussion of budget cuts, Munn was not simply content to list a few. He covered everything that his library did and indicated not only how much cutting had been done but also how much benefit had accrued therefrom.

## Judson Jennings

Jennings of the Seattle Public Library has already been discussed as the foremost proponent of state aid in this sample. He was concerned, as all librarians were, about the depression-caused budget cuts and what he could do about them (R220, R223, R226). His cuts were even more severe because the library was located in a one-industry town, and that industry suffered badly during the early years of the depression. The adult education program in the library was largely a readers' advisory service, and Jennings did his best to maintain it (R224, R232). When the program finally had to close down for a year, he worked hard in getting aid from both the unions and the city to have the service restored. He also worked for the restoration of salaries as early as possible (R230, R233).

Jennings suggested to the profession that certification was going to be required by state aid and saw certification as a major protector of quality (J104). In general, many of the possible invitations to public interference that worried other librarians did not trouble Jennings. He did not see state aid as an occasion for state control of public library service. He did not support federal aid, but only because he did not believe federal aid would increase budgets substantially (J104). Thus, supporting it was not of practical benefit. His concern for quality was expressed in terms of how he could best ascertain that quality be maintained permanently.

*Milton Lord*

On the basis of the evidence available, Lord had two strong interests vis-a-vis the depression: first, reorganizing the Boston Public Library in such a way as to secure the best possible administrative control, and second, reducing the loss of material through vandalism (R19, R20, R21, R23, R24, R26). Lord detailed at great length the administrative structure that he had developed in conjunction with other members of the library staff, indicating how it was to function when funds were available for its implementation. After the funds became available, he spent much time describing the functioning of the new administrative structure, which apparently was a success.

The only other subject to which Lord turned as much attention across the years of the depression was securing the return of library materials and reducing the amount of theft and book mutilation. These distressed him and elicited from the efforts to eliminate them far in excess of the cost of the vandalism itself. A secondary interest of Lord was the amount of salary being paid to the employees of the library. He directed many efforts to the raising of salaries, and as soon as the impact of the depression lessened somewhat, his attention to salaries was immediately rewarded and they were increased (R24, R25).

Negative attention and comment resulted from these increases, however, so much so that Lord felt compelled to devote his entire 1939 report to showing that the increases that he had secured for members of the library staff were justified (R26).

*Carl Roden*

The problems of book supply concerned Carl Roden of the Chicago Public Library, as it did no other librarian in the sample (R50, R51, R53, R54). A lawsuit had held up the collection of all Illinois taxes for eighteen months just before and immediately after the beginning of the depression. Borrowings against anticipated taxes had been excessive in light of what depression taxes subsequently annotated to. Consequently, the Chicago Public Library budget had no funds for books from 1931 to 1935; during that period, book circulation sky-rocketed and then plummeted as the book collection was all but exhausted (R54). The Chicago Public Library's first book money in fifty months was its 1935 state aid allocation of $228,000 (R55). Roden and his staff attempted to make sure that both the branch collections and the permanent collections of the main library were at least partially restored to what they would have been had the purchasing hiatus not occurred. Overall, Roden expressed greatest interest in holding the library together through the depression. Survival, rather than the protection of specific phases of library activity, appeared to be his goal for the Chicago Public Library.

*Adam Strohm*

Strohm was interested, as numerous statements earlier in this study have indicated, in quality. His dominant concern was for getting good books into the hands of the users of the Detroit Public Library, who needed them at the time the need was felt (R86, R91). He did not have the resources to attempt mass circulation to a large population, nor did he show interest in having such resources for that purpose. On the other hand, his belief that good books are always useful to all readers was dominant in his reports and articles. He believed in recreational reading, as he stressed on numerous occasions, but he insisted on good books, not on trash (R91). He did not at any point discuss the contributions to the Detroit Public Library of the various federal work relief programs. His comments on state aid were limited to one, expressing a hope that further efforts would produce more of it (R88). He had nothing, whatever, to say about federal aid in his annual reports. He was interested in getting a living income for his workers but did not insist on that interest. Always, he talked about service, trying to put it into areas where it would be used as he felt libraries should be used. At every step, he attempted to make budget cuts as undamaging as possible to the library. His reports indicated that in general, he succeeded.

*Malcolm Wyer*

Wyer was interested in adult education, perhaps more than in any other subject. He decried budget cuts, and did what he could to defend the Denver Public Library from them. He tried to cut service and establish fees in the most painless manner possible. He talked about and appreciated the contributions of the various federal agencies to the work of the Denver Public Library. But always, his focus, in both annual reports and articles, was on the contributions made by the library in raising the education level of the people the library was established to serve. His major contribution in this area was in insisting that libraries work with all other local agencies in developing education programs for adults, and that they not limit themselves to the one agency set up for adult education, but rather work with churches, lodges, YMCA and YWCA, and every other group that might be interested (J199).

*Harold Brigham*

Brigham of the Louisville Free Public Library was more interested in staff, salaries, and pensions than he was in any other subject and more, perhaps than any other librarian interested in these subjects.[136] He believed it to be the responsibility of library directors to see to it that staff salaries were maintained. In this effort he was, he felt, swimming against the current, for a survey in 1931 had found library leaders uninterested in salaries paid library workers (J21). In 1931, he wrote rather bitterly on the ability of libraries to hire very good people for pittances, simply because so many people were competing for so few openings (J24). As a contributor to the development of the American Library Association-Metropolitan Life Insurance Company pension annuity program, he urged that library directors secure participation by their libraries as a fringe benefit for employees or, where that could not be,

---

[136] See Appendix IV-A p. 189.

that employees join as individuals (J29). He evidences no fear of federal dollars bringing federal control to libraries. The only implication of federal control that he saw was certification, which he thought would conduce to improved service quality (J27). He saw the distinction between professional and subprofessional librarians as necessary and insisted on the need for professional training for professional people (J30). For this reason, he opposed the training class, which he believed tended to break down the distinction and to produce some badly trained librarians and some over-trained clerks to the great detriment of the salaries of both (J32).

*Charles C. Compton*

While still assistant to Bostwick at St. Louis Public Library, Compton was, for 1934-35, elected to the presidency of the American Library Association. Lydenberg, in 1932-33, had preceded him in being so honored while still an assistant.

During Compton's tenure as president, the Association endorsed the principle of federal aid to libraries; he wrote frequently supporting that endorsement. Indeed, no other librarian in the sample wrote so often in favor of federal aid, nor so convincingly. As might be expected, he was also interested in library budgets, writing often to encourage librarians in their efforts to raise them.

As a long-time member of the ALA Committee on Salaries, he encouraged the raising of library salaries, often drawing attention to the unfair discrepancies between library salaries and those in other professions, such as teaching.

CHAPTER FOUR 121

*Carl Vitz*

Finally, Carl Vitz, who directed both the Toledo and the Minneapolis public libraries during the depression, was interested in the development of the science of library administration. His sole comment on the subject was that librarians were still grouping for the basic principles that would inform the practice of librarianship eventually (J178). He was concerned with the development of support for federal aid and stood behind Carlton Joeckel's suggestions firmly (J179). His other interest, public relations, has already been described earlier in this study. Vitz' importance as a writer and director was clearly shown in the fact that the American Library Association selected him to edit and contribute to its handbook on public library finance problems in the depression.[137]

*Summary*

Chapter Four has been concerned with the categories to which the directors turned their attention and with the directors who paid the most attention to the categories. It was assumed at the outset[138] that they wrote about the matters of greatest concern to them. If that assumption is valid, they were most concerned with the work done for their libraries by workers sent to them by relief agencies, the demand for books, the demand for services, adult education, reading interests of library users, and budget. Their comments on each of these categories had a depression bias; that is to say, what they had to say was different

---

[137] Carl Vitz, ed., *Current Problems in Public Library Finance.*
[138] See Chapter I, pp. 6-8.

from what it would have been had there been no depression. The reason is obvious in the area of relief agency contributions and budget, for had there been no depression, relief agencies and severe budget reductions would not have existed. Comments on the demand for books, like the demand itself, seemed to have varied directly with employment levels. Discussions of the demand for services did the same, except less dramatically. Adult education programs gained new impetus as libraries strove to help adult readers to cope with depression-caused problems. Interest in reader interest areas seemed to increase as changes in interest occurred rather than as book demand fluctuated.

Many matters drew less attention then get more now; cooperation among libraries, library planning, recruitment, the relation of the public library to other types of libraries, unemployment of librarians, the role of women as administrators, public relations, service to special groups, and state aid have gained interest. Others, which did attract some attention then, are less interesting today; concern with economic theory is rarer now than in the thirties. Interest in NRA codes passed with the NRA. Concern for fees and economies vary with local economic conditions. Some categories held a moderately high level of interest: salaries and fringe benefits, personnel, federal aid to libraries, service to unserved populations, the use of facilities and vandalism seem not to gain or lose substantially. They attracted their small amount of attention then; they attract it now.

Further consideration of some of these matters, and the conclusions to be derived therefrom, are the concern of the next chapter.

*Chapter 5*
Results and Recommendations

The depression had an impact on the large public libraries that provided this dissertation its statistical base. During the thirties, the directors of the libraries expressed their concerns regarding much of the impact. The statistics relating to the categories of the content analysis measure some of the concern.

Chapter IV has discussed many of the statistics relating to the categories of the content analysis. It is important to qualify any comment on them with the statement that most of the discussion of Chapter IV had, of necessity, to treat each category in isolation—to consider it as a discrete measure of a limited portion of the universe. The hypotheses and objectives of the dissertation required further analysis and examination of relations among the data developed by the content analysis in order to test whether the study succeeds in meeting its objectives.

A comprehensible discussion of those relations requires first of all a restatement of the limitations and of some constraints imposed by content analysis technique. The limitations were of three sorts: time period, sources, and universe. The time period created no problem: for purposes of the dissertation, the depression began on 1 January 1930 and ended on 31 December 1940. This limitation created no difficulties of any kind because the statements that were made regarding the depression's impact started to appear after the opening date and stopped before the closing date—by a matter of months in both cases. The sources, annual reports and journal articles, will be discussed at greater length in the Recommendations section. Suffice it to say here that the two formats contained as much material as was to be found on the subject of the depression's impact on large public libraries. As to the universe, the directors of the nation's largest public libraries were chosen for the stature of their positions, the ease of identification, and the simplicity of definition of the universe. Further, these directors were selected because it was believed that they, more than any other group of public library people, would speak to the other members of the profession with an authority unmatched by any other possible universe.

The methodology imposed technical rigor on both the researcher and his approach to his materials. Content that did not fit into any of the categories could not be coded; hence the categories had to allow for any relevant information that might be encountered during the analysis phase of the research. The coding form forced on the researcher a strict adherence to a technique that unvaryingly permitted no deviations from encoding information—frequently at the price of first searching for it. On the other hand, that requirement meant that information in a paragraph that could not be encoded as a part of the category tended to be lost for content analysis purposes, for there was no way to record the datum of its existence. Consistency demanded, however, that some such rule be followed lest the body of coded information become unmanageably large. Hence, the best available compromise between too many irrelevant data and too few data of any significance was accepted and followed.

The decision to use annual reports has already been the subject of some comment. Annual reports supplied three times as many comments as did journal articles. But the reports supplied only about twice as many detailed discussions. Further comment on that decrease will be made where appropriate.

*Testing of Hypotheses*

This study was undertaken with four hypotheses:

(1) that the depression affected the public library, its services, operations, and policies
(2) that library directors made adjustments in services, operations, and role to enable the library to stay within available revenue and meet changing needs
(3) that federal and state government activity elicited an increasing volume of written responses from the library directors
(4) that the depression affected the attitudes of the directors of large public libraries toward the role of the public library as an institution and toward the public it served.

Only the fourth hypothesis could not be tested by the methodology used in the study. The data were too limited in quantity for an accurate assessment of attitude, and the procedures used were not geared to the psycholinguistic, computer-based studies currently used for the development of such data. The author also did not wish to be drawn into the controversy over the role and scope of content analysis in such studies, a controversy that began as early as 1959,[139] is presently furiously raging, and

---

[139] Work Conference on Content Analysis, *Trends in Content Analysis*, ed. by Ithiel de Sola Pool (Urbana: University of Illinois Press, 1959), pp. 2-3.

seems nowhere near resolution. Such studies of director treatment or key words like "public" or "service" or "library" or any combination of them in series would require the use of computer technology in a manner that would expand this study far beyond its initial range and scope.

With the other three hypotheses, the journalistic model used for the study was effective. The next few pages will indicate something of the nature and extent of that effectiveness.

(1) The Depression Affected the Public Library, Its Services, Operations, and Policies

This hypothesis was the easiest of the four to demonstrate. Budget figures and circulation statistics alone attest to this correlation.[140] The words of the directors, added to the statistics, support the hypothesis that the depression did directly affect the public library, its services, operations, and policies.

(2) Library Directors Made Adjustments in Services, Operations, and Role to Enable the Library to Stay Within Available Revenue and Meet Changing Conditions

*Meet Changing Conditions*

This second hypothesis was tested to the extent that the directors discussed reductions and increases in services. And as was noted above, they discussed reductions reluc-

---

[140] See Appendix III-E, p. 185.

tantly. Such comments as there were reflected a step-by-step reaction to budget cuts, as the reactions were necessary. Adjustments were of a practical, day-to-day nature, as events dictated them, and not usually philosophically or theoretically-oriented. Occasionally, a director made recommendations about cuts, but after he had made his own budget reductions. No director indicated that contingency plans were available to cover a sever fund reduction. When better economic conditions made budget increases possible, no director indicated that a program to return matters to pre-depression levels had been planned for post-crisis implementation. Further, while directors generally endorsed buying cheap reprints to meet the need for some kinds of fiction, none commented on the paperback books that appeared in the latter part of the decade in greater abundance than ever before. The adjustments that were made, then, came within the limits imposed by long practice.

The directors did accept certain role-changes that were thrust upon their libraries by a changing society, but there was no evidence that the directors sought, encouraged, or anticipated the changes. Except for Malcolm Wyer in Denver, who made an effort to develop adult education through the library, comments in this universe by these directors did not indicate a major effort directed toward adults who were out of work. The unemployed came to the library and the library did its best to help them, using programs it already had. Children's service had to be expanded because more children were using the library, but no new efforts were made, except in the District of Columbia, where Bowerman did not want children's service to fall into the hands of the schools.

(3) Federal and State Government Activity in Library Areas Elicited an Increasing Volume of Written Response from the Library Directors

That one director's practice might differ from another's was indicated by their responses in the area of the third hypothesis. There was no flood of response, at least from these directors. Others outside the sample commented vitriolically, voluminously, and continuously on the idea of federal involvement in library activity. The directors in the sample were largely temperate, adopting a wait-and-see attitude, and then waiting for further developments in Washington. Only Beatrice Winser expressed strong beliefs opposed to government activity.[141] Only Charles Compton continued to urge professional activity to secure federal aid, and no one of the librarian-directors, once they had stated their position, apparently chose to continue discussing federal aid. And only one director, Judson Jennings, really advocated state aid.

*Testing Objectives*

The study succeeded in testing three of its four hypotheses and finding adequate data for a number of comments. The next matter to require attention is the extent to which the study met its objectives. The objectives were stated at length in Chapter I.[142] Briefly, they were as follows:

---

[141] See Chapter IV, p. 90.
[142] See Chapter I, pp. 5-6.

CHAPTER FIVE 129

(1) To study the impact of the depression on the internal operations of the library
(2) To find out how and where the depression affected library services
(3) To learn whether library polices changed as a result of the depression
(4) To find whether directors of public libraries changed their attitudes regarding their libraries, the public, or any other matter as a result of the depression

Beyond question, there were data for each of the first three of the objectives, but none that could be used for the fourth, except inferentially. The researcher resisted making inferences on the fourth objective on the ground that the data would have been as strong for the fourth as they were for the other three. In varying amounts, there were data for the other three objectives.

(1) To Study the Impact of the Depression on Internal Operations of the Library

The directors devoted more of their total attention to concern with Internal Operations (432 mentions out of 611 or 71 percent) than did to either of the other objective areas. In both annual reports and periodical articles, their attention exceeded what they gave to anything else, anywhere else.

*Internal Operations and Library as Institution*

To library operations in conjunction with the library as an institution, the directors devoted 228 of the 432 discussions or 53 percent. Among the 143 discussions that appeared in annual reports, seventy-five, or 53 percent, dealt with the effects of a budget reduction on library administration, forty-one, or 29 percent, with library administration alone, twelve, or 8 percent, with the effects of a budget reduction alone, and twelve, or 8 percent, with the combination of library administration and library organization, with three scattered. The specific events that occasioned these comments were treated in Chapter IV, but in general, in all of them, whether budget reductions were obviously discussed or not, the reason for the discussion was the adjustment that a particular library had been compelled to make as a result of a depression-imposed decrease in resources, a decrease to which the library administration had to make an adjustment.

Much of the same situation obtained with comments in the periodical articles. They were more numerous here than in any other article discussions (eighty-five of the total 203 discussions in articles, or 42 percent). The distribution differed slightly from annual reports, however, in that most of the comment (sixty-six discussions, or 78 percent) was devoted to library administration; a very small amount (thirteen, or 15 percent) to discussion of the effects of budget reductions on library administrations, and only six to discussions of library administration and organization. None was devoted to comment on budget reduction alone. Although, many articles on the subject appeared during the early part of the decade, they were written by librarians who were not part of the sample.

CHAPTER FIVE 131

*Internal Operations and Library in Socio-Political Setting*

When one considers the amount of attention that the categories relating to the library in its socio-political setting attracted (658 comments), over one half, or 50 percent, of the total attention that all of the categories got (1235 comments), one must be startled at the relatively small amount of attention accorded the internal operations of the library in conjunction with that attention (eighty-two discussions or 13 percent). Using the data one might easily, and perhaps erroneously, infer that what happens to a library's administration, its organization, and its budget has no impact on its relations with the people it serves or with the government of which it is a part. A better inference is that directors did not write about the matter.

Less than one half as many discussions in annual reports (sixty-one) of internal library operations occurred in mentions of the library in its socio-political settings as in mentions of the library as an institution (143). Of these sixty-one, thirty-three, or 54 percent, were devoted to the prevailing combination, discussions of the effects of budget reductions on matters of concern to library administrations. The next most popular area was discussion of library administration without mention of budget reduction (seventeen), and finally, comment on budget reduction alone appeared nine times in articles.

As was the case with annual report comments about library operations in their socio-political setting, there were fewer discussions in periodical articles than might have been anticipated (twenty-one). A notable difference is that while the attention in annual reports was spread over three possibilities that in the articles was concentrated: it was mostly concerned with library administration. For whatever reason, when writing for the journals, the directors did not mention their concern with library organization and administration.

*Internal Operations and Economic Conditions*

There was only about one-third as much attention to categories relating to economic conditions (206), as there was to those concerned with the library in its socio-political setting (658). But in director concern with internal operations, the total annual reports and articles under economic conditions exceeded that under socio-political setting, 122 to eighty-two. As usual, comments in annual reports were more numerous (ninety-three annual reports, twenty-nine discussions in articles), mainly because there were more annual reports.

The most popular of the possibilities was comment on the effect of a budget reduction on library administration. Of the ninety-three discussions in the annual reports, fifty-nine, or 63 percent of them occurred here. Of the rest, twenty-one were devoted to discussions of library administration and eleven to discussions of the effects of a budget reduction.

Nearly all of the comment in periodicals was devoted to library administration in one way or another. Sixteen of the twenty-nine discussions were solely on library administration, and twelve of the remaining thirteen were on the effect of a budget reduction on library administration. The result of these data is to be expected in light of the fact that most comment on economic conditions concerned budgets and nearly all of the comments on library operations were ultimately related to administration.

*Generalizations on Concern with Internal Operations*

To draw together in brief compass all of the comments on library operations, especially when it covered so many areas discussed in Chapter IV, is not feasible. Rather, two generalizations emerge: there was more concern with library operations than with either services or policies. A second generalization also is evident: there were more discussions in articles concerning library operations, proportionally, than is usual with the categories. The usual ratio between annual reports and articles is three to one. But there were 33 percent more of these discussions in articles than the usual ratio would lead one to expect. Perhaps one might reasonably have expected the preponderance that developed. Concern with internal operations, especially where budgets were involved, was high, and thus attention would naturally be drawn to that area. Budgetary impact was greatest on such matters as personnel, salaries, book funds, and so forth, where the administrative decisions on resource allocation frequently caused the most discomfort.

(2) To Find How the Depression Affected Library Services

Considering the frequency with which library directors and others mentioned the extent of their concern with library services outside the universe (the listings in library literature were numerous), there were few discussions of services in either of the annual reports (seventy-five discussions). The four to one ratio between concern with internal operations (432) and with services (ninety-eight) is possibly illuminating.

## Services and Library in Socio-Political Setting

One would reasonably expect major concern with services to appear in the treatment of the library in its socio-political setting if that concern is to appear anywhere. However, no such concern surfaces. Only twenty-eight discussions appeared in annual reports, a figure that in itself is discouraging. But of those twenty-eight, more discussed service increases (eleven or 40 percent) than discussed any other single subject or combination of subjects. Next most numerous was the combination of service reductions and the extent of the reductions (seven). Next came service inaugurations (six), and finally, and surprisingly, service reductions (three). On the basis of this evidence, it may be concluded that the directors preferred to talk about the expansion in service rather than the decrease that took place, especially in annual reports. And when they could not talk about increases in service, they frequently kept silent.

## Services and Economic Conditions

Finally, discussions of services were made in conjunction with comments about economic conditions. There were fewer of them than of any other area treated thus far, fourteen in all, including both annual reports and articles. Since there were only ten in annual reports and four in articles, separate treatment was felt to be unwarranted. Predictably enough, when the directors discussed services in the context of economic conditions, they said more about reductions and the extent of reductions than they did about any other area (eight discussions). In second place were discussions of reductions that did not go into their extent (three). In two cases, directors discussed service increases, and in one rarity, a discussion of the extent of reduction was accompanied by another discussion of an increase.

*Generalizations on Concern with Services*

The data on concern with services are too few to permit extensive generalizations. One fourth as many discussions of services as of operations appeared. There were more discussions of increases in service than the generally depressed economy during the decade would seem to justify. Or, perhaps, there were far fewer discussions of service reduction than the facts warranted and the comparison is striking. And finally, services were not discussed in journal articles.

(3) To Learn Whether Library Policies Changed as a Result of the Depression

*Policies and Library as Institution*

Once again the paucity of information requires the combined treatment of what appeared in articles and annual reports. In this area of policy in conjunction with the library as an institution, discussions in articles were more numerous than discussions in annual reports (twenty-one in articles, twelve in annual reports). Of the thirty-three discussions, eighteen or 55 percent, the largest group, were on such policy areas as personnel, book loan policy, and the like. Of the rest, more were on book selection policy (eleven) than on any other. Only adult education policy (three) attracted any other attention.

It is to be noted that these comments were in the area of library operations. Library policies would mostly affect what the library does for its constituency, the socio-political setting of the library so to speak. Reasonably, one would expect to find far more comment on policy in this area.

## Policies and Library in Socio-Political Setting

The expectation of extensive comment on policy in the library in its socio-political setting was not realized. Forty-two discussions of policy occurred under this heading compared to thirty-three discussions of policy under library as an institution. Almost double that amount of concern was shown in the eighty-two discussions of the internal library operations in conjunction with the library in its socio-political setting. Of the forty-two discussions of policy, book selection had six, adult education had six, and temporary unemployment for relief purposes had two. Over 50 percent or twenty-six discussions were individual mentions of different policy matters.

## Economic Conditions

Only six discussions of policy occurred in the context of economic conditions, four of them on book selection policy. The other two were scattered. Again the numbers are too few to allow for conclusions of any validity.

## Lack Generalizations on Concern with Policies

No generalizations may be arrived at on policy from the few data that the universe supplied, or perhaps, in reverse, the library directors did not produce a consensus of comment on policy matters in the materials they wrote in journal articles and annual reports.

*Generalizations Concerning Objectives*

To summarize is really to restate. First, library directors discussed internal library operations (432 of the total 611 discussions) far more frequently than they did any other area. There were over twice as many discussions of operations as there were of services and policies combined. Second, discussions of services were fewer than might be expected until the relatively high number of comments on service inauguration and increase is noticed. One is led to suspect then that the directors may have avoided extended comment on service decreases. Third, there were fewer discussions of policy (81) than there were of services (98), but only by a few. It is remarkable that only among discussions of policy were comments in articles more numerous than those from annual reports (45 from articles versus 36 from annual reports). It is to be noted that in the relatively enormous number of annual report pages that were encoded (3,893 pages), the number of comments concerning policy (36), or less than one per hundred pages, seems to demonstrate very minimal concern on the part of directors. It is evident that policies were not discussed in annual reports, although some policy changes might be noted in passing. Controversial policy changes were apparently not discussed in print although some ideas related to policies were sometimes discussed in periodical articles.

*Summary of Results*

The foregoing discussion of the hypotheses indicates much of what can be stated finally about the findings of this study. A few further generalizations may serve to assemble the most important of the findings.

More comments (658 or 53 percent of the total) about the library in its socio-political setting were made than were made about the library as an institution and economic conditions combined (577). Second, with slightly over 30 percent of all the attention was the library as an institution (371), and economic conditions were third with 17 percent of the total attention (206).

The prevalence of comments on the library in its socio-political setting may be traced to the presence of a number of categories that attracted brief attention—categories such as book circulation, which usually elicited a simple statement that it had either increased or decreased, and demand for services, where much of the same sort of comment was made. Contributions of relief agencies to libraries elicited similar comment, except that frequently a brief note on the nature of the contribution was added.

Comments in the areas treated by categories grouped under the library as an institution were occasionally fuller. The comments that could be encoded for treatment under discussions of services, of operations, and of policies attest to this. Nearly half of all such comment (303 discussions, or 49 percent) was in those areas. The remainder was almost equally divided between discussions in conjunction with the library in its socio-political setting and economic conditions.

Of the comments on economic conditions (206), nearly 75 percent concern budget—reductions and increases

CHAPTER FIVE 139

(147). The rest was scattered among fees and economies, finances, and taxes and taxation.

The extensiveness of the comments on the library as an institution seems to indicate the importance of such concerns to the directors and those for whom they wrote. Personnel, salaries, the library as an institution, and political interference with personnel were accorded attention exceeding that of categories in the other two major areas. In contrast, in terms of fullness of comment, the library in conjunction with its socio-political setting elicited 166 comments out of a possible 68, and economic conditions elicited 142 comments out of a possible 206.

Certain anticipated relationships appeared: it was expected that fluctuations in library operating budgets would reflect fluctuations in economic conditions and that comment on budget would reflect such fluctuations; that book circulation would reflect unemployment and that comment on it would also be in proportion to such unemployment. There was substantial correlation between budgets and economic conditions, such that a budget drop could be expected after failures of businesses increased, especially before the New Deal.[143]

Furthermore, unemployment and book circulation seem to directly parallel each other, as is shown better perhaps than the attrition of book collections would justify at the end of the first Roosevelt administration, when the cuts in welfare programs pushed unemployment upward, for ordinarily attrition would result in a drop in circulation.[144] For years, directors had been saying that collections were wearing out, that soon there would be no

---

[143] See Appendix III-C, p. 183.
[144] See Appendix III-A, B, C, pp. 181-83.

books for anyone to borrow. In 1937, when unemployment increased dramatically, circulation should not have increased because the book stocks were nearly exhausted. But it did, between 1936 and 1937, and again between 1938 and 1939.

An apparent relation between bookstock and book circulation figures seems not to be explainable by any single set of data: bookstock fluctuation was apparently independent of operating expenditures (book expenditures were not uniformly reported and thus cannot be used). Bookstocks apparently reflect data that libraries did not uniformly report and that are not hinted at in annual reports. Changes in the basis of counting and gifts, for example, might have upset the figures. There seems to be a general trend in the same direction, though, between book circulation and bookstock figures, and the fact that apparently contrary assumptions are required to explain the trend does not negate it. (If business failure creates unemployment and unemployment raises book circulation; and further, if business failure causes budget cuts and budget cuts result in drops in bookstock; then circulation increases ought to come at about the same time as bookstock drops. Thus, a longish period of low budgets and high circulation ought to create a substantial drop in bookstock.) Figures,[145] however, do not reflect that specific series of events. Apparently libraries were not discarding books that in better times would not have been kept.

Certain things were not learned: an attempt to relate the total written output of the directors to library size, budget, budget per capita, and total budget failed. There

---

[145] See Appendix III-D, p. 184.

simply were not enough data to justify any conclusions. Some library directors wrote, and others did not. Had low cost sound recording equipment or an oral history project been available during the thirties to save the observations of the otherwise silent librarians, perhaps this study would have had far different results.

*Recommendations for Future Research*

The studies of content analysis that were referred to in Chapter III agree that content analysis technique did not produce new information. The researcher must predetermine what kinds of data he will seek. If those data exist, the application of the technique will find them. If other data exist beside those previously designated, they will almost certainly be overlooked by the researcher whose categories do not accommodate them. In consequence, this study cannot irrefutably claim to have found all relevant material in the public library directors' writings during the depression. However, as was indicated earlier, since the category *Other* was not heavily used, an appropriate category existed for everything in the universe. The data also fitted naturally into the designated categories and were not forced into them. The findings of this study can therefore be relied on as accurate. An independent reliability test was made to check the selection of categories and coding form, and the correlation between tester and researcher was 92.9 percent.[146]

A useful sequence to this study would be to take its findings back to the universe to investigate the most interesting themes that content analysis has indicated. The

---

[146] See Appendix IV-E, p. 217.

themes relating to personnel (political interference, salaries, unions, and unemployment), the themes of planning and cooperation, and the special problems in Ohio and Illinois was taxation that so disrupted public library service could well merit further scholarly investigation. Local library files, newspapers, and even transcripts of local radio programs, if they exist, might be valuable.

At no point has this study attempted to break new ground in the technique of content analysis. The current trends toward the use of computers in psycholinguistic analysis of communication are far removed from the analysis of themes; that was the concern for this research, hence they were not used. The journalistic models in content analysis were used and they served well. A future study, however, may well use the psycholinguistic approach of content analysis to investigate the promising and complex fields involving the attitudes of public library directors toward the public, the library, federal funding, and other agencies of government, whether during the depression or some other significant time block.

The journalistic models in approaching content analysis functioned best in isolating categories and in pointing out unproductive portions of the universe. The application of the technique has shown how best it could be applied in future studies, and some of the problems encountered in this present study could thus be avoided. Ruling out annual reports that contained only brief comments and omitting non-productive types of article comments such as signed committee reports, brief signed notices, book reviews, and attributed comments would probably improve the universe of a future study. It might be worthwhile also to enlarge the universe by reducing the population base; library directors such as Orlando Davis of Bridgeport, Connecticut, Samuel Ranck of Grand Rapids, Michigan, and Ida Wright of Evanston, Illinois, whose libraries served over 50,000 people, but who published frequently, might be included. Limiting the types of articles to speech texts, signed full-scale articles, editorials, and letters to the editor might provide better coverage of well-developed statements and eliminate many of the comments that were undeveloped. A future investigation might consider treating the materials in annual reports in a universe separate from another universe using journal articles, for this study found that mixing the two frequently provided confused results that required explanations that might not otherwise have been necessary. The material in annual reports was more dilute; it was frequently unqualified with modifying material; it has to be accorded treatment different from that given material in articles.

Treatment of the categories might be altered somewhat for future studies not related to the depression. First, a decision could be made to ignore any category that failed to attract a minimum of attention; this would remove much of the diffuseness that appeared in Chapter IV. Second, the categories relating to economic conditions could be assigned to the other two groups to achieve greater clarity; treating concern with budget and economies as facets of the library as an institution, and concern with service fees, finances, and taxes and taxation as part of the library in its socio-political milieu would give better balance to the thesis. Adjustments for passage of time and language changes could also be made, for the categories that evolved from this depression study could easily lend themselves to other library studies.

Two final recommendations concern universe and categories. First, librarians who had not achieved director status during the depression decade, but were to do so later, or were otherwise to distinguish themselves by, for example, publication or academic accomplishments, might provide valuable comment on the categories of this study. Special areas where their contributions might be sought are departmental budget reductions and their implications, salaries, personnel problems, and library unions from the subordinate's viewpoint. Second, certain categories are potentially interesting even though they attracted little attention from this sample of librarians. Those categories are library policy of public libraries on a broad basis, and federal aid to libraries, as a hotly debated issue. Study of any of these problems could amply reward the effort and scholarship any such study would entail.

## Appendices

The appendices are available online at:

http://libraryjuicepress.com/kramp-appendices.php

Appendix I – Primary Sources
Appendix I A – List of Libraries With Directors Who Served in the Years 1930-1940
Appendix I B – List of Librarian Authors
Appendix I C – Annual Reports
Appendix I D – Articles by Librarian Authors

Appendix II – Materials Related to Content Analysis
Appendix II A – List of Categories
Appendix II B – Coding Form

Appendix III – Charts

Appendix IV – Results of Analysis
Appendix IV A – Category by Author
Appendix IV B – Author by Year
Appendix IV C – Category by Year
Appendix IV D – Distribution of Discussions
Appendix IV E – Reliability

# Bibliography

American Library Association. Special Committee on Library Aid. "Libraries and Federal Aid." *American Library Association Bulletin* 30 (May 1936): 421-71.

Berelson, Bernard. *Content Analysis in Communication Research.* Glencoe, Illinois: Free Press, 1952.

_____. "Library Unionization." *Library Quarterly* 9 (October 1939): 497-510.

Berry, John. Telephone interview. To *Library Journal* , 11 April 1975.

Brogan, Denis. *Era of Franklin D. Roosevelt.* Chronicles of America Series, vol. 52. New Haven, Connecticut: Yale University Press, 1950.

Budd, Richard W.; Thorp, Robert K., and Donohew, Lewis. Content Analysis of Communications. New York: Macmillan Company, 1967.

Chancellor, John. *Library in the TVA Adult Education Program.* Chicago: American Library Association, 1937.

_____. *Printed Page and the Public Flatform.* United States Office of Education Bulletin 1937, no 27. Washington, D.C.: Government Printing Office, 1937.

_____, ed. *Helping Adults to Learn: the Library in Action.* Chicago: American Library Association, 1939.

Deily, Robert H. "Public Library Expenditures in Cities of over 1,000,000 Population in Relation to Municipal Expenditures and Economic Ability." Ph.D. dissertation, University of Chicago, 1941.

Duffus, Robert L. *Our Starving Libraries.* Boston: Houghton Mifflin, 1933.

Flexner, Jennie M., and Hopkins, Bryon C. *Readers' Advisers at Work: A Survey of Development in New York Public Library.* New York: American Association for Adult Education, 1941.

Galbraith, John Kenneth. *Great Crash, 1929.* Boston: Riverside Press of Houghton Mifflin, 1954; Sentry Edition, 1961.

Haygood, Wiliam Converse. *Who Uses the Public Library; a Survey of the Patrons of the Circulation and Reference Departments of the New York Public Library.* Chicago: University of Chicago Press, 1938.

Herdman, Margaret M. "Public Library in Depression." Ph.D. dissertation, University of Chicago, 1941.

Hicks, John. *Republican Ascendancy, 1921-33.* New American Nation Series. New York: Harper and Row, 1960.

Joeckel, Carleton B. *Government of the American Public Library.* Chicago: University of Chicago Press, 1935.

_____. *Library Service.* President's Advisory Committee on Education, Staff Study no. 11. Washington, D.C.: Government Printing Office, 1938.

Johnson, Alvin. Public Library—a People's University. New York: American Association for Adult Education, 1937.

Leland, Simeon. "Observations on Financing Libraries." Library Quarterly 2 (October 1932): 344-66.

Leuchtenberg, *William E. Franklin D. Roosevelt and the New Deal.* New American Nation Series. New York: Harper and Row, 1963.

Merrill, Julia Wright; Estes, Grace W.; Chancellor, John; and Milam, Carl H. "Library Projects under FERA." *American Library Association Bulletin* 28 (October 1934): 823-39.

Mitchell, Broadus. *Depression Decade: From New Era through New Deal.* Economic History of the United States Series Vol. IV, New York: Henry Holt and Company, 1947; New York: Harper and Row Torchbook Edition, 1969.

"National Plan for Libraries." *Library Journal* 59 (September 1, 1934): 661-63.

"National Plan for Libraries, As Revised and Adopted by the A.L.A. Council, December 29, 1938." *American Library Association Bulletin* 33 (February 1939): 136-50.

"Public Library and the Depression." *Wilson Bulletin for Libraries* 6 (December 1931): 267-68.

Purdy, George Flint. "Public Library Services in the Middle West." *Library Quarterly* 8 (July 1938): 346-72.

Reeves, Floyd W. *Adult Education.* New York: McGraw-Hill, 1938.

Schlesinger, Arthur Meier, Jr. *Age of Roosevelt.* 3 vols. Boston: Riverside Press of Houghton Mifflin, 1957-60.

Shepard, David Wakefield. "Experiment in Content Analysis: the Radio Addresses of Henry J. Taylor, 1945-50." Ph.D. dissertation, University of Minnesota, 1953.

"Should Libraries Unionize?" *Library Journal* 62 (August 1937): 587-93.

Stanford, Edwards Barrett. "Library Extension under the W.P.A.: an Appraisal of an Experiment in Federal Aid." Ph.D. dissertation, University of Chicago, 1942.

"State Aid Policy Question." *American Library Association Bulletin* 30 (September 1936): 887-91.

Stone, Philip J.; Dumphy, Dexter C.; Smith, Marshall S.; and Ogilvie, Daniel M. *General Inquirer: a Computer Approach to Content Analysis.* Cambridge, Massachusetts: M.I.T. Press, 1966.

Vitz, Carl, ed. Current Problems in Public Library Finance. Chicago: American Library Association, 1933.

Waples, Douglas; Carnovsky, Leon; and Randall. William M. "Public Library in the Depression." *Library Quarterly* 2 (October 1932): 321-43.

Wecter, Dixon. *Age of the Great Depression, 1929-41.* New York: Macmillan Company, 1948.

Wilson, Louis Round. *Geography of Reading: a Study of the Status and Distribution of Libraries in the United States.* Chicago: American Library Association of the University of Chicago Press, 1938.

Work Conference on Content Analysis. Trends in Content Analysis, edited by Ithiel de Sola Pool. Urbana: University of Illinois Press, 1959.

# Index

American Association for Adult Education, 69
American Library Association, 3, 11, 23, 38-39, 82-83, 89-90, 105-106, 120, 121
   negroes and, 86-87, 105
     *see also* library services
   women and, 87, 122

Bowerman, George F., 112-113
Brigham, Harold, 119-120
budgets, 25, 27, 34-35, 49, 62, 71-74, 75-76, 77-78, 94, 96, 99-101, 108-109, 112-113, 115-117, 119-122, 126-127, 130-133
   salaries, 25, 27, 34-35, 75-76, 78, 80-81, 98-99, 110, 115-116, 119-120, 122

circulation, 66, 75
   adult fiction, 26, 65, 66, 71, 78, 95, 127
   adult nonfiction, 26, 66, 78, 95
   juvenile, 26
   juvenile nonfiction, 26
   movies and, 26
   patron reading interests, 62-63, 70-71, 78, 121-122
   unemployment effects on, 26, 43, 65
     *see also* New Deal
     *see also* unemployment
     *see also* World War II
     *see also* library service
Compton, Charles C., 120
content analysis, 51-53, 54, 59, 105, 123-125
   assumptions and, 7-8
   coding form and, 56-59, 124
   hypothesis and, 8-9, 123, 125-126, 128-129, 138
   limitations of, 9-11, 123
   objectives of, 5-7, 123, 128-129recommendations for future research in, 141-144summary of results of, 138-141
   universe and, 7, 52-54, 57-59, 62, 106, 123-124, 127

directors,
   reduced finances and, 6-7, 10, 27, 36
     *see also* federal aid to libraries
     *see also* state aid to libraries
   reduced staff and, 6-7, 79-80
   demand for books and, 6-7, 27, 62, 66
   demand for services and, 6-7, 27, 62, 67

expenditure,
   book expenditures, 25-26

total expenditures, 25-27
binding, 25, 35, 85-86, 91
maintenance, 25, 35
*see also* library service

federal aid to libraries, 28-30, 36-41, 48-49, 78, 88-90, 111-112, 114, 116, 118, 120-122
*see also* state aid to libraries
Ferguson, Milton J., 111-112

Galbraith, John Kenneth, 10
Great Depression,
book stores and, 26, 45
book rental agencies and, 26, 45
impact on directors attitudes, 6-7, 17, 27, 53, 106, 123, 127-128
*see also* directors
impact on internal operations, 5, 129, 133, 137
impact on library budgets, *see* budgets
impact on library policies, 6, 133, 136-137
fine cancellation, 56, 96-98, 110
impact on library services, 6, 33, 43-45, 49, 67, 68, 133
*see also* library services
*see also* public libraries
impact on public libraries, 2-6, 12, 17, 19-20, 23-24, 33, 35, 48, 52, 55, 92-93, 123-124
radios and, 26

historians,
Leuchtenberg, William E., 1, 2-3, 15-16
Mitchell, Broadus, 1, 3, 12-14, 15, 19
Schlesinger, Jr., Arthur Meier, 1-2, 22
Wecter, Dixon, 1, 3-4
Hoover, President Herbert, 14-15, 16

Jennings, Judson, 115-116

labor unions,
*see* library unionization
Leuchtenberg, William E., *see* historians
library, elementary school, 77, 113
library budgets,
*see* budgets
library circulation,
*see* circulation
library directors,
*see* directors
library expenditure,
*see* expenditure
library personnel, 78-79, 122
political interference and, 83-85, 105
library services,
adult education and, *see* public libraries
children, youth and, 94, 109, 111, 113, 127
circulation and, 32, 34
*see also* circulation
expenditures and, 31-33, 35, 100

negroes and, 22-23, 31, 32, *see also* American Library Association
*see also* Great Depression
Library Services Act, 30, 41
library unionization, 22, 41-42, 82-83, 110, 115
literature review, 25-33
Lord, Milton, 116-117
Lydenberg, Harry Miller, 107-109, 120

Mitchell, Broadus, *see* historians
Munn, Ralph, 114-115

National Labor Relations Act, 41
New Deal, 16, 18-20, 23, 37, 62, 63, 71, 80, 89
  Agricultural Adjustment Act (AAA), 14
  Civilian Conservation Corp (CC), 18
  Civil Works Administration (CWA), 14, 17, 18, 28, 63, 64, 65, 108
  Federal Emergency Relief Administration (FERA), 18, 28, 36-37, 63, 108
  National Industrial Recovery Act (NIRA), 14, 22, 41, 83
  National Recovery Administration (NRA), 20, 91
  National Youth Administration (NYA), 14, 19, 63, 108
  Public Works Administration (PWA), 14, 18, 91-92
  Tennessee Valley Authority (TVA), 18, 46
  unemployment and, 28-30
  *see also* circulation
  *see also* unemployment
  *see also* World War II
  Works Progress Administration (WPA), 14, 19, 27-30, 63, 64, 65, 84, 85-86, 94, 108, 112

public libraries,
  adult education and, 45, 46-49, 62-63, 69-70, 98, 107-108, 115, 118-119, 121-122, 127, 135
  negroes and, 69
  as an institution, 1, 75-81, 103, 129-130, 136
  as a social and political institution, 4, 88, 131-132, 134-136

Roden, Carl, 117
Roosevelt administration, 3, 17, 20
  *see also* New Deal
  *see also* Roosevelt, President Franklin Delano
Roosevelt, President Franklin Delano, 13-15, 16-17, *see also* Roosevelt administration

Second World War,
  *see* World War II

Schecter decision, 20
Schlesinger, Jr., Arthur Meier,
    *see* historians
Sherman, Clarence, 109-111
state aid to libraries, 36-41,
    48-49, 78. 88-89, 92, 100-
    102, 111, 114-118, 122,
    128
    *see also* federal aid to libraries
Strohm, Adam, 118

unemployment, 81-82, 127
    *see also* circulation
    *see also* New Deal
    *see also* World War II
unions,
    *see* library unionization

Vitz, Carl, 121

Wagner Act, 22, 83
Wecter, Dixon,
    *see* historians
World War II, 1, 10, 14
    unemployment and, 10
        *see also* circulation
        *see also* New Deal
        *see also* unemployment
Wyer, Malcolm, 118-119

www.ingramcontent.com/pod-product-compliance
Lightning Source LLC
Chambersburg PA
CBHW060836190426
43197CB00040B/2652